SB   R 9.95 G
     11/04/94 SA

1.56

Canoeing in South Africa

Rory Pennefather

SOUTHERN
BOOK PUBLISHERS

Dedication

To my wife, Jane, who provided me with ideas and helped make decisions throughout the writing of this book.

The following photographers contributed to the colour photos: John Oliver, Val Adamson, Alick Rennie, Tim Biggs, Jerome Truran, Danie Coetzer.

The following photographers provided black and white photos: John Oliver, Val Adamson, Alick Rennie, Tim Biggs, Rowan Sampson, *The Natal Witness.*

Copyright © 1991 by R. Pennefather

All rights reserved. No part of this publication may be reproduced or transmitted in any form or by any means without prior written permission from the publisher.

ISBN 1 86812 363 4

First edition, first impression 1991

Published by
Southern Book Publishers (Pty) Ltd
PO Box 3103, Halfway House, 1685

Cover photograph by The Portrait Place
Cover design by Michael Barnett
Design by Etienne van Duyker
Illustrations by Rina Coetzee
Set in 10$^{1}/_{2}$/11pt Century Schoolbook
by Unifoto Cape Town
Printed and bound by CTP Book Printers, Cape

Canoeing in South Africa

ACKNOWLEDGEMENTS

Many people helped me with this book; in fact very little of it is solely my own creation. I am greatly indebted to a number of people.

Firstly, without my mother and father my metamorphosis into a canoeist would never have taken place. My mother was always willing to finance my canoeing schemes and was my first opponent in canoe racing. The fact that she had a galvanised iron bath and I a racing K1 meant that I always won and consequently grew to love the sport.

My father spent his middle years transporting my brother and me to canoe races around the country, and even the theft of his suitcase during the Duzi marathon, which forced him to spend the rest of the race in his pyjamas, did not dim his enthusiasm.

My parents also bought the computer with which I was able to write this book.

Several photographers went to endless trouble to obtain excellent pictures, particularly John Oliver, Val Adamson, Alick Rennie and Tim Biggs, who provided me with most of the photographs used in the book. I am particularly indebted to John Oliver for the trouble he went to in getting the specialist pictures I needed and for making copies of the pics I used from other photographers.

Tim Biggs provided the article in Chapter 9 on canoeing rivers in the western Cape and waterfall photographs.

Graeme Pope-Ellis gave valuable advice and information on the Duzi and his Duzi training programmes.

Peter Peacock wrote the piece on sprint training in Chapter 4 and Mark Perrow provided his training log on the Berg River marathon of 1990 and a description of canoeing rivers in the Transvaal.

Dr John Godlonton gave helpful information on all health aspects, including bilharzia, dehydration and hypoglycaemia.

Richard Turnbull provided help and advice on training in the gym, and also assisted with photographs of the exercises.

Alick Rennie gave advice and shared his schedule for slalom training.

Nigel Tatham read through the book in its early stages and offered advice and suggestions.

FOREWORD

This is the encyclopaedia of canoeing in South Africa. It is the first book to explain every aspect of this adventure sport, from which canoe to buy and which paddling technique to use, to where to find the rivers and dams. It covers, in depth, long distance racing, white water, sprinting, slalom and tripping, how to handle flat water, roaring rapids and even waterfalls, in clear and exciting English. Although most of it is technical, it is spiced with anecdotes.

Rory Pennefather, a Springbok canoeist, is one of the best all-round paddlers South Africa has ever produced. Rated as one of the world's top long distance paddlers, he has competed in most junior European events and is probably better equipped for the job of writing this book than anyone. He has taken part in all four disciplines of the sport at the highest level, and has represented his country in two of them: long distance and white water. He has conquered most of South Africa's major rivers, either racing competitively or leisurely tripping, admiring the fantastic scenery and playing in the rapids.

Where Rory Pennefather has felt an inadequacy in his own expertise, he has called in other writers such as Tim Biggs, Mark Perrow and Peter Peacock. This gives the book a universality which would otherwise not be attainable.

Obviously this book is aimed at beginners, those adventurous young men and women yearning to pit themselves against nature, but it also speaks to the mid-fielder struggling to upgrade his or her performance. This book could make the difference between winning and coming second and will definitely form a part of my collection.

Graeme Pope-Ellis

CONTENTS

Introduction

1 Equipment 1
Kayaks 1
   Plastic (tupperware) canoes 1
   Slalom kayaks 2
   Wild water racers 3
   Racing singles (K1s) 4
   Racing doubles (K2s) 5
   Four-seaters (K4s) 7
Other equipment 8
   Paddles 8
   Wings 9
   Pumps 10
   Spray covers 12
   Life-jackets 12
   Helmets 13
Clothing 15
Repairs 16
   Patching 16
   Other repairs 17

2 Will canoeing suit me? 20

3 Technique 23
Style 23
   Holding the paddle 23
   Sitting position 23
   Body movement 25
   Stability 26
   Turning 26
Flat water techniques 27
   Paddling a straight course 27
   Wave riding 27
   Mistakes to be avoided 28
The K2 29
   Turning a K2 30

River long distance   30
   The fastest channel   30
   Avoiding sand banks   30
   Using the current   31
   Resting in rapids   31
Wild water techniques   31
   The low telemark   32
   The high telemark   32
   The high brace   33
   The draw stroke   34
   The sculling brace   34
   The sculling draw   37
   The bow rudder   37
Using the current   39
   Breaking in   39
   Breaking out   40
   Ferry gliding   40
The ender   42
The Eskimo roll   44
   How to roll   44
   Some important points   44
   Learning to roll   47
Paddling continuity   48

4 Training   50
Interval training (sprint repetitions)   53
Gym work   55
Flexibility   56
   Some stretching exercises   57
Weight training for strength   64
Recommended training programmes   71
   Duzi training programme *Graeme Pope-Ellis*   72
   Training for sprints *Peter Peacock*   75
   Long distance training *Mark Perrow*   78

5 Sprints   81
The 500 m   81
The 1 000 m   82
The 10 000 m   83
Successful sprinting   83

6 Wild water racing   85
The racing line   86
Pacing   87
Warming up   87

7 Slalom   91
Slalom training *Alick Rennie*   94

8 Long distance racing 99
The Duzi marathon 100
   The choice of canoe 102
   Other equipment 103
   Duzi training 105
   The race 106
The Umkomaas 108
   How to paddle in the Umkomaas 108
   The Umkomaas marathon route 109
   River sections 110
The Berg River marathon 114
The Breede 117
The Fish 117
The Vaal 119
The Jukskei and Highveld Crocodile 119
The Lowveld Crocodile 120
Shorter long distance events 120
Relay races 120

9 Where to go canoeing 122
Natal 125
   Easy sections for the beginner 125
   Sections for those with a bit of experience 127
   Sections for the more experienced 128
   Sections for the experienced white water tripper 131
   The Tugela 132
Transvaal 133
   The Highveld Crocodile *Mark Perrow* 133
   The Vaal *Mark Perrow* 135
Cape Province 136
   The western Cape *Tim Biggs* 136
Transkei 139

10 White water tripping 141
Waterfalls 143
Rapids 143

11 Canoeing triathlons 150
Weekly training 151
The long-term training scheme 152

12 Surf and sea 153
Surfing 153
Off-shore paddling 155

13 Safety 156
Dangerous situations 158
  Man-made obstacles 158
  Natural obstacles 160
Equipment 163
What can go wrong? 164
  Swimming in a rapid 164
  Being held in a stopper 165
  Being trapped in a kayak 165
  Injuries 165

14 Health 167
Dehydration 167
Hypoglycaemia 167
Injuries 168
Bilharzia 168
  Guidelines for management 168
Sun protection 169
Diarrhoea 169
Canoeist's "sciatica" 169
Cramps 170

15 Other aspects of canoeing 171
The environment 171
Social responsibility 172
Canoeing action 174
The lure of canoeing 175
Duzi fever 177
The future 177

Glossary 179

Index 181

INTRODUCTION

The warm, muddy water engulfed me as I plunged into yet another stopper. Water strained on the spray cover, pulling down on the straps, before the boat sprang back onto the surface. The long line of standing waves stretched before me, marking out the route the boat was to follow. Cliffs rose steeply on all sides as the river snaked its way through the endless hills.

My canoe moved swiftly, carried relentlessly by the current, responding magnificently to the paddle. Narrowly skirting large rocks and holes, I manoeuvred my canoe nerve-rackingly close to danger. In the flooding river the rapid was several kilometres long, leaving no alternative but to keep going.

The final drop loomed ominously ahead, and a thundering stopper blocked the centre of the river. Paddling furiously to the left, I skirted the hole with less than an inch to spare and was deposited in a deep, calm pool.

This memory of a January day on the Umkomaas is just one of the many thrilling memories from my own canoeing experience. Every time I take to the water, a unique and special atmosphere is created, for every river has its own moods and character. A river is not an inanimate object, continuously spilling water into the sea, but a living being that can be benign or furious; forgiving or stern. The paddler is particularly fortunate for he is one of the few people who ever has the opportunity to experience the diversity of emotions evoked by a wild and free-flowing river.

Canoeing is a sport with so much diversity that some aspect of it is bound to appeal to almost everyone. Canoes, too, vary considerably so that anyone who is really serious about the sport will have several different boats. On my last count I had 14 lying about the garden. It's not enough but I make do, using the one that is most suitable but never perfect for the conditions.

The cheapness, versatility, light weight and durability of canoes account for their popularity. Unlike larger boats, canoes are easily carried by the paddler and transported on the roof of a car. They can be used wherever there is water and are ideally suited to the steep and shallow streams which abound in this country. Canoeing is one of the most popular water sports in South Africa and is growing at such a rate that it is becoming a major national sport. There are in excess of 4 000 canoeists registered with the South African Canoeing Federation (SACF) and the number is growing continuously. There are also hundreds of paddlers who are neither registered nor involved in racing, so the number of canoeists in the country is far larger than this.

Correctly speaking, paddlers in South Africa are kayakists and not really canoeists at all. The term "canoe" refers to the Canadian or Red Indian boat which is propelled by a single-bladed paddle, whereas any boat which is navigated with a double-bladed paddle is termed a kayak. This makes all the boats used in competition, rough water tripping and sea "canoeing", kayaks. However, the word "canoeing" has become so firmly entrenched in South African English when discussing kayaking that it is the term I will use in this book. The term "kayaking" will be used only when differentiation between canoeing and kayaking is necessary.

International sporting isolation and warm, rough rivers have been responsible for the unique way in which canoeing in South Africa has developed. The emphasis, even in racing, is on pleasure, with the best of flat water paddlers spending much of their canoeing time in rough water. Using K1 and K2 craft, which are considered highly unsuitable for white water, the average South African paddler has developed into an extremely competent rough water canoeist. Although behind many countries in sprint and slalom canoeing, South Africans are possibly best in rough water long distance racing.

With the growing interest in canoeing in South Africa, paddlers and would-be paddlers have been in search of information about how to tackle the sport. This book hopes to provide some of the answers and generate interest in one of the most enjoyable and exciting outdoor pastimes that there is.

1 EQUIPMENT

Kayaks

The uses of kayaks are extremely varied and there are consequently a considerable variety of designs. No single design is perfect for all applications so most active canoeists own several different canoes. Choosing the right canoe for your interests and demands can be a confusing task, so it is best to have a good idea of the types that are available.

Some paddlers compromise their choice of canoe and try to buy a general purpose design in order to enjoy a little bit of everything, but in reality no general purpose design exists. A broad canoe is slow and stable, a narrow canoe is wobbly and fast; a long canoe is fast but does not turn well, a short canoe is manoeuvrable but slow. You cannot have your kayak and eat it!

When choosing your first canoe it is wise to consider what your priorities are. With time, as your canoeing interests diversify, you can always buy a second boat — avoid selling the first one if possible. Canoes are like money; you can never have too much or too many.

Plastic (tupperware) canoes

These short, stable, virtually indestructible canoes are designed mainly with rough water canoeing in mind. Their shapes vary from competitive slalom types to short polo-bat models. The longer designs are slowly losing popularity as expert rough water paddlers are now favouring the

Plastic kayak. (John Oliver)

shorter boats. These are exceptionally manoeuvrable, but inclined to loop end over end very easily; something which the expert actually wants! A beginner would do well to start off in a medium-length model, but the design is not critically important at first. Canoeing without leaks and not having to do any patching more than make up for an unfashionable design.

The tupperware canoe is a highly suitable rough water boat. It has revolutionised river canoeing, making steep and rocky mountain streams navigable. If one decides to portage a waterfall (not always necessary in one of these boats), it is always possible to slide down the side and into the water below.

Initially the price of plastic canoes was rather high compared to glassfibre boats, but local production has made them much more affordable.

Slalom kayaks

These boats are designed with manoeuvrability as the top priority. Consequently a slalom boat has a flat-rockered hull so that it spins like a saucer. The decks are also very low in order to skim under slalom poles and speed up the turning process. The edges are very sharp, giving the boat an angular appearance. All this makes it a small, responsive and exceptionally twitchy machine. It has very little buoyancy so that looping happens all too easily, and in some ways it is not really suitable for the rough water it is used in. It is the right design for the competitive slalomist, but the buoyant plastic and old-fashioned slalom boats are more suitable for general rough water paddling.

Slalom kayak. (John Oliver)

Wild water racers

Perhaps the wild water boat is the one which comes closest to being an all-purpose canoe. It combines speed, manoeuvrability and stability in varying degrees and is used for racing down rough river sections. Speed through rough water is the designer's top priority, but as these boats have no rudders, they have to be manoeuvrable. To paddle them fast in large rapids the paddler has to be stable, so consequently a small amount of speed will be sacrificed to increase stability.

The modern wild water racer is often specifically designed with one section of river in mind, usually the course for the forthcoming world championships. If the rapids are straight and small, the boat will be sleek and fast, similar to a flat water racing K1. If the world championships course is very rough with twisty, demanding rapids, the boat is made more stable and turns well. The latter type is more pleasant to paddle and is often used for trip canoeing and canoe camping because it has plenty of room for storing kit.

The lack of a rudder makes turning difficult at first, but as wild water racers are half a metre shorter than racing singles, steering becomes easy once mastered. Rudders are sometimes fitted but the foot controls take up valuable storage space. A rudder can also give trouble in rough and rocky conditions, and as it is not really necessary, is better left off.

The above three types have small white water cockpits. This means that you are squeezed into them with your knees firmly locked in place underneath the deck. They also allow for the wearing of totally waterproof neoprene spray covers. Such a cockpit is essential for the execution of an Eskimo roll. Some paddlers fit knee braces, hip pads, and back belts so that they fit snugly in their boats. Every movement of the pad-

Wild water racer. (John Oliver)

4 Equipment

The white water cockpit; small and snug with hip pads and back-strap. (John Oliver)

dle is transferred directly to the canoe, improving boat control. Many novices are frightened off by these small cockpits, afraid that they might be trapped upside-down in them. If you have such fears, take your boat to a swimming pool and try falling out. By relaxing and pushing yourself out backwards, you should float out very easily. Falling out is always easier than you think!

Racing singles (K1s)
The single racing kayak is the most popular canoe in South Africa. It is fast, responsive, sleek and very unstable, used for both calm water sprinting and river long distance racing. Its ability to glide along effortlessly, its quick, light responsiveness and good turning by rudder make it popular. To the novice, its lack of stability is totally unmanageable, but perseverance is rewarded by the smoothest ride a canoe can give.

Most racing K1s are designed in Europe solely for flat water racing so the low decks and narrow noses are not ideally suited to the rough rivers in which they are used in this country. In good hands they perform surprisingly well in very large rapids and are used to the exclusion of almost all other designs in all rough water long distance races in this country.

If you are planning on sprinting or racing the Berg River marathon or a similar flat water race then go for the latest and sleekest designs. But if you are new to the game and planning to do some river canoeing, then choose from the more stable models. There is a large variety available which can make choosing difficult, but the Lancer derivatives and other similar designs are a fair amount more stable than the newer models and not all that much slower. If you are heavy and inexperienced, start in the most stable K1 available.

Various modifications have been done to racing K1s, such as the fitting of high decks for more buoyancy and the moulding of small cockpits to facilitate Eskimo rolling.

Racing doubles (K2s)

These boats, almost as popular as the K1s, are favoured particularly in the long two to three-day marathons, for their comfort and speed help them to eat up the miles. A good crew in a moderately flowing river can hold a speed of 15 km per hour, making the racing double a very efficient means of transport in rough country.

Double designs are similar to those of the singles, with sister models built along the same lines. This means that if the Tiger K1 suits you, for example, then so should the Tiger K2.

Beginners carrying a bit of weight would do well to use the stable Accord-type boats, but if they are lighter or prepared to work hard at it, the Foxbat, Mirage and Tiger designs would be more suitable. The latter three are fairly stable and fast, bridging the gap between the Accord and the very twitchy sprint designs. Only change to these modern

Racing K1. (John Oliver)

6 Equipment

Racing K2. (John Oliver)

sprint boats once you are sufficiently stable or if you are planning on doing flat water canoeing.

The more experienced paddler should sit in the front of a K2, for it is his job to make the decisions and to steer the canoe. It is thus more tiring than sitting in the back so it helps if the front paddler is also the fitter of the two.

This does not mean that the canoeist in the back seat should have an easy time, for it is his job to provide the extra power when it is needed in rapids and to help with the steering when called upon to do so by the man in front.

A good understanding and a large amount of tolerance are called for in K2 canoeing for it is a sport that often lands one in tricky situations. When the front paddler sees disaster looming, he is inclined to shout rather desperately for action from his partner. This must not be construed as criticism as it is usually desperately necessary advice, or a result of fear. The two of you are in the same boat, so if your partner is terrified, he obviously knows something you don't! The best thing you can do is to obey orders and ask questions afterwards. The front paddler should, however, learn to master irritation, and give instructions in a constructive manner so that no offence can be taken.

K2s provide a different experience in canoeing. When prospective canoeists deliberate on the choice between a double or single, I always advise on the use of a K1 at first. In this way one becomes competent oneself. It is then worthwhile trying out a double. But it should not be seen as a choice between singles and doubles; one should paddle both for they provide different canoeing experiences. Use singles in some races and doubles in others. By sharing expenses with a friend one can cut costs drastically and afford to own both types.

Four-seaters (K4s)

The K4 is the fastest kayak in the world. With four pairs of paddles propelling it along, it cruises at an incredibly high speed, covering a kilometre in little more than three minutes. Timing is of critical importance and if it is correct the boat glides along effortlessly. If it is just slightly out, the boat feels sluggish and unwieldy.

K4s are used for flat water paddling only. They encourage team-work and generate club spirit as most K4 races are inter-club or inter-provincial events. They race over all sprint distances and are also used in long distance races of two to three hours' duration.

K4s using the wave in a long distance race. (Val Adamson)

Other equipment

Paddles

The kayak paddle has two blades set at right angles to each other. This is called feathering and facilitates an easy paddling style while reducing wind resistance on the blade as it is pushed forwards. Paddles can be set with either a left or right feather. This determines whether the shaft is controlled by the left or right hand, with the paddle continually swivelled in the other hand.

Using a left or right-feathered paddle has nothing to do with whether one is left or right handed, and a beginner could learn to use either, but once the habit is formed, a change is very hard to make.

Right-feathered paddles are most commonly used and I would recommend them, for if you break your own paddle, it is easy to borrow a replacement.

The blade of a racing paddle is asymmetrical. This stops it from twisting in the water as equal areas of blade are submerged on either side of the central rib as the blade enters the water. The shorter edge of the blade should therefore face downwards (see figure 1.1).

With a general purpose paddle, the shaft is inclined to twist as the blade enters the water, as force is exerted on one side of the blade only. But symmetrically shaped blades have their advantages and are used especially in slalom and other canoeing activities where many backwards and sideways strokes are used.

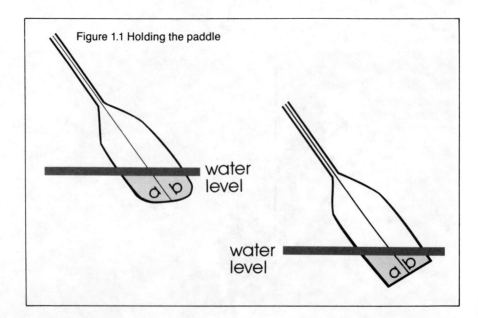

Figure 1.1 Holding the paddle

Wings

A new concept in paddles materialised in the early eighties with the advent of "wings". These peculiarly shaped blades resemble a hollow aeroplane wing. They decrease friction on the back of the blade, creating a smoother, more efficient action and a slight increase in canoe speed. They also get a better grip on the water so that less water can slip off the sides of the blade, which loses power. "Free power" is also gained from the blade as it enters the water, as it tends to slip forward. By simply holding onto the blade, the paddler is pulled forward with it, thus gaining a minuscule amount of distance.

Wings also help to correct some of the most common errors of style. This makes them of particular advantage to advanced paddlers who have developed poor technique over the years. Technical errors of style are eliminated by the natural action of wings. They do, however, seem to work best with strong paddlers, and once a canoeist is tired and his style deteriorates, they are possibly slower than conventional blades.

Lacking a flat back surface makes the slap-support stroke difficult and fairly deep water is required for them to operate properly. This makes wings of dubious advantage in South African river conditions, but anyone who plans to sprint or race on calm water should definitely try them. Within a decade there will be few sprint and long distance paddlers who do not use wings.

Paddle length varies from 2 to 2,25 m, and is dependent upon the height of the paddler and the proposed use of the paddle. Length is always referred to in centimetres; for example a paddle is called a 216 or 221, this being its length in centimetres.

The paddle blades of four different models: from left to right: struer, slalom, wings, standard. (John Oliver)

Sprint and long distance paddles are relatively long, ranging from 217 to 225 cm. The following table should be used as a rough guide only, as paddle length is also affected by strength, a strong paddler using a paddle longer than that recommended here.

Height of paddler		**Length of paddle**
165–170 cm	(5 ft 5 in–5 ft 7 in)	215–218 cm
170–175 cm	(5 ft 7 in–5 ft 9 in)	217–220 cm
175–180 cm	(5 ft 9 in–5 ft 11 in)	220–223 cm
185 cm+	(6 ft and taller)	222–225 cm

Many paddlers vary the length of their paddle; I find that the fitter I get the longer the paddle I like to use. A shorter paddle feels better in a river which is shallow or very full for this eases the force on the arms which has been increased by the drag or strong current.

Slalom paddles range from 200 to 210 cm; wild water blades are usually 214 to 218 cm long. The thing to remember when choosing a paddle is that length is not critical while you are learning. As long as your blade is not excessively short or long, it will work well. The only way of finding the correct length paddle for you is to paddle as often as you can, and then to decide for yourself what suits you best.

The most prestigious paddles were once made of wood, but these are virtually now obsolete as kevlar, foam and other synthetic materials have taken over. Wooden paddles can still be obtained, usually imported, but the resilience and lightness of modern materials make them more than a match for wood.

Pumps

Pumps are used extensively in long distance races such as the Umkomaas marathon, where large waves pound on the spray covers for hours on end. Operated electronically or by the paddler's foot, they pump out any water that leaks into the boat.

Pumps can give trouble: valves jam with dirt, pipes come loose and switches malfunction on battery-operated ones. It is therefore best to fit two pumps to your boat so that at all times one pump is likely to be in operation.

Electric pumps are exceptionally fast at pumping water out of the boat, but they are expensive, the batteries go flat and electrical problems can occur. They also do not get the boat as dry as foot-operated ones, so a combination of the two is perhaps best.

Pumps are most necessary in K2 craft as water leaks in through two cockpits. By fitting them to the back footrest, the front paddler is left free to control the rudder while the back paddler operates the pump.

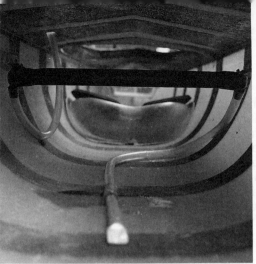
The Lendal foot pump. (John Oliver)

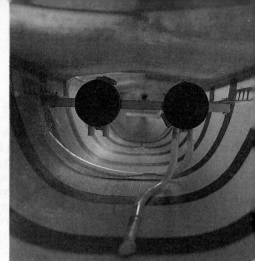
Two concertina pumps being fitted to a K2 back footrest. (John Oliver)

The neoprene spray cover fits tightly around the paddler and the cockpit. (John Oliver)

Spray covers

After the canoe and paddle, the spray cover is the next most important item of equipment for the canoeist. It is used primarily to keep your boat dry, but also provides warmth in cold conditions. It attaches the canoeist to the canoe with a body tube around the paddler's waist and a broad skirt-like section attached to the canoe-cockpit coaming.

Spray covers for plastic, slalom and wild water racers are small in order to fit the smaller cockpits. The best quality ones are made of neoprene and are extremely waterproof.

Larger spray covers made of plastic material and waterproof nylons are used on racing singles and doubles. Before buying a spray cover, make sure it fits your canoe. Some doubles have particularly large cockpits and a standard spray cover may be too small. It should be tight enough to prevent pools of water from building up in folds in the material, but loose enough to allow free body movement.

They are elasticised around the waist and the edge which fits onto the cockpit rim, and should have shoulder straps to prevent them from slipping down under the weight of waves. These straps are inclined to slip off the shoulders unless they are crossed on the back.

Life-jackets

A life-jacket is a vital but often neglected item of equipment. Besides providing assistance in the event of a capsize, it helps keep the canoe

A small life jacket leaves the paddler unhindered but does not give much support to a swimmer. (John Oliver)

The jacket-type buoyancy aid provides more help when swimming. (John Oliver)

waterproof by forming a barrier to waves which would otherwise come crashing down on the paddler and leaking into the boat.

Some life-jackets provide very little buoyancy and are used mainly to make the racing paddler legal. These models should obviously be avoided in big water, although they do leave the paddler unencumbered, an obvious advantage in wild water racing and slalom.

Life-jackets that appear large and cumbersome provide excellent support for a swimmer and have the added advantage of affording padding against rocks for a capsized paddler in a shallow river.

Helmets

A helmet is one of the most necessary items of equipment for the rough water canoeist. There are numerous models on the market, some of which do little more than make you legal in racing, while others could save your life.

Besides the obvious function of protecting your head against rocks, a helmet can protect you from swinging slalom poles, clashing paddles in congested races, skis and boards in the surf and even your own canoe if you happen to fall out and swim down a rapid with your boat.

Cheap helmets with holes for ears or no sides and no protection for the temples are little more than a waste of time. A large, well-padded helmet

14 Equipment

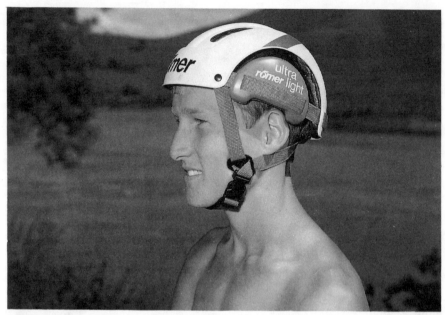

Such a plastic helmet offers little protection and leaves ears and temples exposed. (John Oliver)

A popular polycarbonate model provides good protection if adjusted to fit properly. (John Oliver)

This full, well-padded model is comfortable and protective. Ears are free but not exposed to rocks. (John Oliver)

actually improves one's rolling for one can hang upside down and let the helmet bash against the rocks until one is ready to roll up. It is impossible to remain calm upside down in the water when your ears are being ripped off and your forehead beaten in.

The combination of a good life-jacket and helmet is like a suit of armour. The capsized paddler is able to roll forward against the front deck of his boat and let his protective clothing take the beating while he prepares for his roll.

Clothing

South Africa's weather is near to perfect for the canoeist. The majority of the country experiences warm, wet summers, providing full, warm rivers and sunny skies. This means that most canoeing can be done with the paddler free from layers of heavy, restrictive clothing. There are some garments, however, which make the canoeist comfortable and help to keep his canoe dry.

Canoeing shorts are designed along the lines of cycling shorts and protect the paddler from chafing on the canoe seat. They are also made of synthetic fibres which dry very quickly.

Triathlon suits are a development from canoeing shorts, consisting of a vest and shorts suit all in one. This is the ideal garment in which to paddle, cycle, run and swim, as it remains comfortable and light even when it is wet.

Anoraks are necessary in cold, wet weather such as occurs in the western Cape in winter. The warmer rivers of the summer rainfall region seldom call for them, with a long-sleeved T-shirt usually being all that is required during a cold snap, especially if you are paddling hard or racing. It is advisable to carry one in the boat with you if you are tripping and spending a full day out on the river.

The cold conditions overseas have resulted in the designing of some excellent anoraks which will keep one warm in near freezing water. Tight neoprene collars and cuffs keep out the cold and the water.

Thermal vests, commonly referred to as "hally hansons", provide excellent warmth especially when wet. Available (from overseas) with short and long sleeves, they are ideal for racing in cold weather and tripping on cool days, for they keep one warm while avoiding the restricting feeling of layers of clothes.

As far as **footwear** is concerned, canoeists working rudder controls usually prefer to paddle barefoot, but this is near impossible if any portaging is required. Light running shoes are tolerable and about the best bet, but in cold weather where portaging is minimal wetsuit booties are more suitable.

Repairs

There was a time before the early seventies when most — if not all — canoeists had to build their own boats. Commercial builders were non-existent, so if you wanted a canoe you had no alternative but to build one yourself.

With the advent of canoe shops and factories, the need to build one's own canoe ceased. Well-built modern designs became readily available, and even the efficient do-it-yourselfer found it increasingly difficult to keep up. Club moulds deteriorated and designs became outdated. Commercial craft took over to such an extent that few paddlers today know how to make a canoe.

Building your own canoe would certainly save some money, but not as much as you might think. You would pay a high price for your materials as you are not buying in bulk and there is a fair amount of wastage. The lack of good available moulds together with the trial and error way of learning means that the quality of your first home-built canoe would not be very good. But if you are a handyman with a desire to build your own canoe, it is worth giving it a try. Building your own canoe is indeed one of the satisfying challenges of the sport.

Although the canoeist of the 1990s does not have to know how to build his canoe, he does have to know how to work with fibreglass, as patching is one of the inevitable consequences of canoeing. The type of job that might need to be done can range from patching a small hole to joining a boat completely broken in two.

The versatility of glassfibre is such that the parts of two broken canoes can be joined together to make one good boat again. I have previously cut out the centre of a badly damaged K2 and joined the back and front together to make a successful K1. Such drastic and large jobs are seldom necessary, however, and most canoe workshops are prepared to do the more difficult repair work. But patching small holes that result from general wear and tear are best done by the canoeist himself.

Patching

To do the most basic patches you will need the following:

(a) Materials
    1 m chopped strand fibreglass matting
    50 ml catalyst
    1 kg resin
    500 ml acetone or thinners

(b) Tools and equipment
    rasp, file or sandpaper
    1 paintbrush
    2 tins: one for mixing resin, one for washing the brush

These materials are more than is needed for one small patch and are probably sufficient to do several repair jobs, but it is difficult to buy smaller quantities. Having extra fibreglass is not a waste, for as inevitably as full rivers follow rain, canoes get holes.
1. Before a hole can be patched, the area must be completely dry and clean. Using either a sanding pad on an electric drill, coarse, effective sandpaper or a good rasp, roughen the area around the hole for at least 5 cm on all sides.
2. Pour approximately 100 ml of resin into a jam tin and add 1 to 2 ml of catalyst. The hotter it is, the less catalyst you need to use.
3. Mix the resin and catalyst thoroughly, then paint the hole and roughened area with resin.
4. Place a small patch of chopped strand mat over the hole and impregnate it with resin, using dabbing strokes with the brush. (This first layer should be smaller than the second layer.) More resin than is required for the patch can be used as it will be absorbed by the second layer.
5. Apply a second layer approximately the same size as the roughened area around the patch. Do not make it bigger than this area or the edges will not stick properly to the boat.
6. A third layer should only be applied to extremely large holes or if you plan to sand the patch smooth. This should be done, but is not practical when patches are applied on river banks or at overnight stops on marathons.
7. The dry, smooth patch can then be painted to match the boat and no sign of the damage remains. Do not use just any paint but rather one suited to boats. One disadvantage of paint is that it has to be cleaned off if another patch needs to be applied, and if it flakes, it slows the boat down by increasing drag in the water. Gelcoat (a thick surfacing resin) is often used as it waterproofs and protects the patch. It can be coloured to match the boat. Only a thin coat need be applied.

Clear hulls are easily fixed with invisible patches and can simply be painted with clear varnish to hide the sanding scratches once the patch is completed.
8. Wash the brush in acetone or thinners. All resin must be removed from the brush or it will slowly harden.

Other repairs
By keeping a thorough check on your equipment, most repair work can be avoided. The following items should be checked regularly, i.e. before races or long trips:

- Rudder cables — Are they tight or could they slip loose? Have they any weak points?
- Nuts — Make sure all nuts on seats, rudders and pedals cannot work loose.
- Paddles — Are blades still stuck in?

18 Equipment

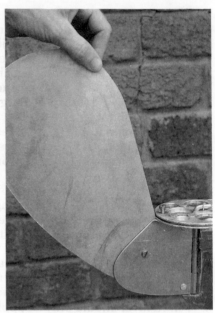

The rudder mechanism. (John Oliver)

The rudder blade flips up when bashed by rocks or weirs. (John Oliver)

Pedal controls to turn the rudder. (John Oliver)

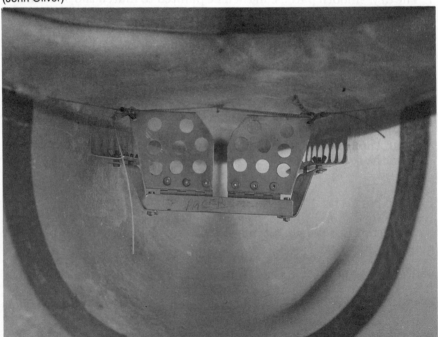

A K2 negotiates the Cradock weir, last obstacle in the Fish River marathon. (John Oliver)

Mark Perrow and Neil Evans take on Goodenough's weir on the Umkomaas marathon, one of the more daunting obstacles in the race. (Val Adamson)

An 'ender' in a K2; the Umkomaas claims another victim. (Val Adamson)

Spanish sosatie — Herman Chalupsky braces himself to take the blow of an angry Spanish paddler in a long distance race in Spain. "You smasha my boat; I smasha your face!" (Photographer unknown)

- Seats — Are they still strong and are the fittings onto the boat still firm?
- Spray covers — Are they tear-free and waterproof? Are the shoulder straps still secure?

You should also check the boat for holes and weak points after paddling in the river and especially at overnight stops during marathons. They are not always that obvious, only becoming noticeable when you start sinking the following day.

2 WILL CANOEING SUIT ME?

The stereotype canoeist is a large, muscular male with massive shoulders and biceps, a fearless stare, and more strength than brain. Nothing could be further from the truth. The top men paddlers range from 55 to 110 kg. The best of them are sometimes beaten by scrawny 15 year olds or outclassed in the river by petite young women. In fact, canoeing is a great leveller, for technique, training, experience and energy conservation are just as important as sheer strength.

This makes canoeing the ideal sport for almost everyone. If you want to be good you can be good. All it takes is time and perseverance. One of the greatest pleasures in canoeing is improving, for every enjoyable trip down the river is part of the learning experience. So the more often you go out and have fun, the better you become.

Unlike running, canoeing does not jolt the body or jar muscles. For people who have injuries or carry excess weight it has many advantages. Besides helping one to shed a few kilograms, the canoe, rather than the legs, carry the extra load. A bit of fat can even be an advantage, for it acts as an energy store in a long race.

Initially women make better canoeists than men. Their broader hips and narrower shoulders lead to good stability as their centre of gravity is lower. Being lighter, their canoes float higher, which is better in the shallows, and a novice woman is less inclined to capsize a double than a novice man. There is less effort required for an experienced paddler to right a K2 if it is thrown off-balance by a light partner than a heavy partner. With time, however, men catch up, but it takes a lot more effort in the early stages.

Children, like women, have the advantage of light weight and good balance, and once they can swim, they can canoe. Several designs such as the Nipper, polo-bat and various slalom models are ideal for youngsters. Under experienced supervision children as young as 10 can shoot small rapids. There is little as memorable as the experience of shooting your first rapid, and doing this at a tender age makes it that much more enjoyable.

South Africans generally take up canoeing in adulthood. Apart from the few schools that now offer the sport, few children have access to the expensive equipment and transport needed for the sport. This is a pity as teenage years, when canoeing could be so greatly enjoyed, pass by wasted (in a canoeing sense of course)! This is where we could learn from Britain, where many children as young as 10 go down to the river on weekends and mess about in boats. The boats are owned and stored by clubs, so access to canoeing is not limited to children from more affluent families.

South African canoeing is far more "capitalistic". The need for transport and individual equipment places it out of reach of many young would-be canoeists. There are also not many boat houses on waters, or coaches to provide the necessary back-up for young paddlers. If we hope to improve our racing standards, much more time and money need to be spent on coaching and assisting youngsters.

The suitability of canoeing for people of all shapes and ages has led to the inclusion of several classes in long distance racing. These include juniors (under 19 years); seniors (20 to 37 years); veterans (38 to 49 years); masters (over 50 years); and women.

Several different K2 classes have also been created. These apply especially to the Duzi marathon. Some of these are father and son; mixed double (man and woman); novice; and novice and experienced paddler. Other combinations which have raced on the Duzi include father and daughter and mother and son teams.

Indeed, there is no combination that does not work in a double canoe. Some might be faster than others, but all are capable of becoming competent and providing pleasure. The double is the best way of introducing novices to the sport for they can sit in the back cockpit and get a ride down a river, enjoying all the efficiency of the experienced paddler in the front. It is also a good opportunity to learn correct techniques from the skilled partner. However, a single should not be neglected for it is here that one gets the chance to test and improve one's own skill.

The combination of a man and woman in a K2, the mixed double, is an exceptionally popular racing class. It is in keeping with the family tradition of South African canoeing and opens the sport up to female paddlers who might otherwise stay at home or spend a day driving along river banks.

It is generally believed that the woman gets the better deal, for she benefits from a strong and experienced partner, but the man too can gain. Some women are exceptionally skilled and light with a good strength to weight ratio; they are usually more stable than men and have better natural stamina. Even an inexperienced girl is usually sufficiently stable and light for a man to pull a double along virtually on his own.

Usually in mixed doubles racing men have the experience and talk inexperienced girls into paddling with them. This has led to the belief that mixed doubles is more of a social than a racing class, but as more women become skilled paddlers, the number of competitive mixed doubles is growing dramatically. A top mixed double is capable of competing against some of the best men's crews and is often seen in the top 10 in results lists. What I have always liked about paddling with my wife is that she knows exactly what must be done in order to save time and energy. We are able to train together continually, thus timing, turning and stabilising are worked on every time we paddle and consequently improve.

One problem that besets some mixed doubles pairs is the matter of balancing the weight. Ideally the lighter paddler should sit in the front of a K2. In most cases this is the woman. However the more experienced paddler is also the one that should be in front and usually this is the man. Generally the heavier male sits in front and the slight drop in performance from having the weight unevenly distributed is ignored. I have seen a mixed double rigged up with the footrest pedals mounted on the back footrest so that the male paddler was able to steer the boat from the back cockpit. This meant that the weight was correctly distributed and the more experienced paddler steered. This is a steering method that is unorthodox and not recommended, for few paddlers are capable of steering successfully with the limited view from the back.

Mixed doubles classes are now included in all K2 races with the Underberg race on the Umzimkulu being the only exclusively mixed doubles race. It consequently introduces many women to the sport. This has both its positive and negative aspects for many girls are enchanted by the race but an equally large number vow never to venture near a canoe again. This all depends on the approach that mixed doubles teams have to the race.

The race covers the section from the trout hatcheries to the Coleford Bridge (described in Chapter 9). Here the river flows through some of the most beautiful countryside in Natal.

Preparation makes the difference between an idyllic day out and a "Deliverance" style nightmare. If you are planning on paddling the race with a beginner, give him or her the chance to try out canoeing on flat water before the race. Pass on a few basic tips, provide good equipment and don't play the cowboy in the rapids. A confident and cautious approach, especially in the rapids of the gorge, is the safest policy. If the boat feels unsteady, give in to a subconscious desire to portage the bigger rapids.

3 TECHNIQUE

Although the various forms of canoeing differ considerably, there are certain techniques which are common to all aspects of the sport. All canoe designs have their own peculiarities and react differently to the paddle, but the basic reaction is essentially the same. A racing kayak is, for instance, far less responsive to turning strokes than a slalom boat, but more responsive to forward strokes. A canoeist who has learnt to use a paddle effectively in one type of canoe, however, can adjust to other types with a fair amount of success in a relatively short time. The slap-support stroke is, for example, an effective stabilising stroke irrespective of the design canoe you are in.

Style

An efficient paddling style is the key to canoeing success. One saves a great deal of energy if one uses the paddle properly. Every stroke should be long, straight and smooth, but before style can be perfected, the paddler must make sure that he is holding the paddle correctly and sitting in the correct position in the boat.

Holding the paddle
Your hands should grip the paddle slightly wider than shoulder width (see Figure 3.1). Wrists should always be held as straight as possible, although the twisting action due to the feathering makes it impossible to keep them perfectly straight. Do not grip the shaft too tightly as this leads to sore forearms. The paddle slips or rotates in the left hand and is twisted by the right (if you are using a right-feathered paddle). The grip in both hands can be relaxed during the pushing action. This relaxes the forearms. (Paddles can be left or right feathered, the latter being the most common. See Chapter 1 on equipment.)

Sitting position
The seat should be positioned approximately 2 to 3 cm off the bottom of the boat. The higher it is, the easier it is to get a straight hard pull in, but a high seat increases instability. For paddlers still learning to balance a canoe, it helps to remove the seat for a while. In this way the centre of gravity is lowered and the boat feels steadier.

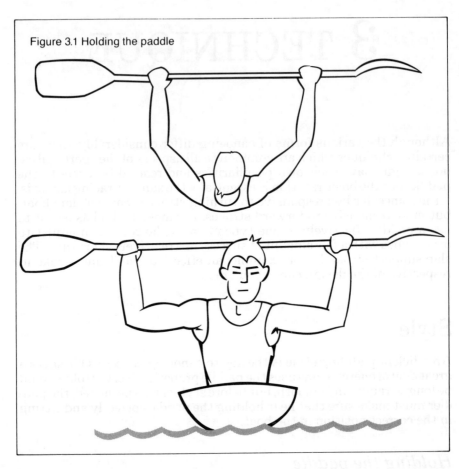

Figure 3.1 Holding the paddle

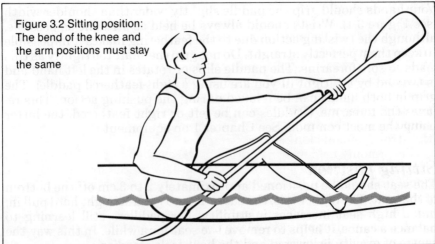

Figure 3.2 Sitting position: The bend of the knee and the arm positions must stay the same

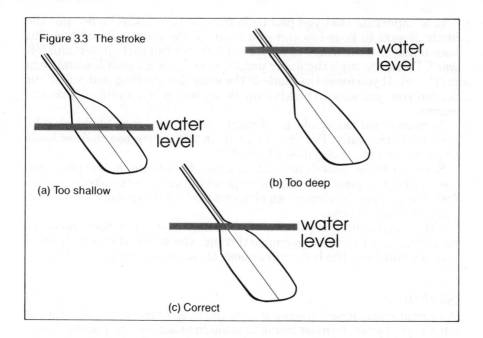

Figure 3.3 The stroke
(a) Too shallow
(b) Too deep
(c) Correct

The feet must rest on the footrest so that the knees are slightly bent, just protruding above the cockpit. In this position the paddler can use the footrest to push on, which assists the twisting action necessary for strong, hard strokes. It also helps to keep stable and eliminates the rocking action of the boat. The average distance of the footrest from the front of the seat is about 80 cm.

Body movement

Trunk rotation and arm extension form the basis of good kayak paddling technique, for paddling is mainly a pulling exercise and the further forward the arm is extended, the longer the pulling action can be. With one arm extended, the paddler drops the blade into the water and draws himself up to it using a powerful pull and trunk rotation. One should not lean forward in order to lengthen the stroke, as this leads to a bobbing action which is tiring and causes excessive bouncing of the canoe. By simply straightening the upper arm, the paddler ensures that the stroke remains long and efficient.

A commonly held misconception is that a good push with the upper arm improves the efficiency of the stroke. This is not true. Certainly the upper arm must not lie idle, but pulling is the action which is most important in paddling. You cannot pull if you are really working on pushing, but make sure that you are extending your upper arm to its full stretch before dropping the blade into the water. This will ensure that your paddle stroke is as long as possible.

It is important that you paddle in front of your body; do not put the blade in next to your hip and pull it out of the water behind you. Put your blade into the water as far forward as you can without leaning forward. Pull it through the water until it is in line with your hip and then pull it out. If you leave the blade in the water for too long and pull it out behind you, you end up picking up water, which is a waste of time and energy.

To ensure that the stroke is efficient, the whole of each blade must be inserted in the water. Putting the blade in too deep or too shallow leads to an inefficient stroke. (See Figure 3.3.)

Style can be perfected only with practice. Make sure that no peculiarities start developing. If you are not splashing and your stroke feels comfortable, you are developing an efficient style. Always work on perfecting it during training.

Efficient paddling requires a smooth movement. The boat must not rock from side to side or porpoise through the water. If every stroke is smooth and long, the boat will appear to move along effortlessly.

Stability

As already mentioned, the removal of the seat increases the stability of a boat, but by far the most important aid in balance is the paddle. Never let go of it; it is your balance bar and support. Stability improves naturally with practice, but the paddle used well helps the paddler to stay upright in the most wobbly of craft. Every time the paddle is pulled through the water it stabilises the paddler. There are also several strokes that can be used to keep the paddler upright or help him regain his balance should he lose it. The most valuable of all these is the *slap-support*.

The slap-support stroke is, as its name suggests, a slap on the surface of the water. As the boat falls off balance, the paddler rests the *back of the blade* on the surface. The leading edge of the blade must be held above the water, giving the blade a water-ski type action. This lifts the blade and gives the paddler something to lean on. It follows that the faster the canoe is going, the more uplift one gets from the blade. If one is not going very fast, one sweeps the blade forward to increase the force of the water under the blade and hence its lifting action.

A paddler sitting still will never hold his paddle out of the water, but skim it continually to and fro to provide him with something to lean on.

Turning

With a racing kayak, turning is a simple matter. K1s, K2s and K4s are fitted with rudders which do most of the work for the canoeist, but a few basic turning strokes are still necessary to get the boat round in tight situations. Rough water craft such as slalom, white water and plastic boats rely entirely on paddle strokes to turn them.

Turning by paddling close to the boat on one side and far on the other

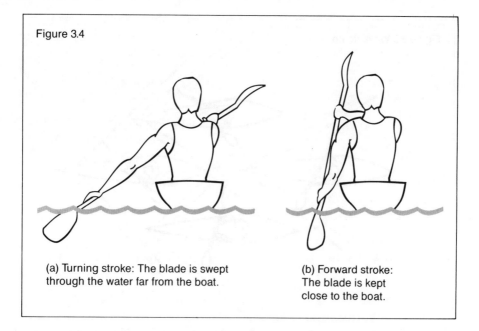

Figure 3.4

(a) Turning stroke: The blade is swept through the water far from the boat.

(b) Forward stroke: The blade is kept close to the boat.

is an effective way of steering a rudderless kayak. A straight stroke close to the boat has very little turning effect, while a curved stroke far from the side turns the boat to the side away from the paddle. (See Figure 3.4.)

Flat water techniques

Paddling a straight course

In many long distance races and some sprint events, it is necessary to cross large, open stretches of water. A large arc can be several metres further than a straight line, so concentrate and make sure that you are travelling as short a distance as possible. Do not blindly follow the group in front of you, for if they are travelling in an arc, it could be your chance to catch up with them. You can also ride on the waves that they are putting up and work your way forward to catch them. In a river where the current is not too strong, the shortest route remains the fastest route. Cut all the corners as much as you can without paddling into shallow water, which is often found on the insides of bends.

Wave riding

This is a technique that any paddler who spends a certain amount of time training or racing learns automatically. Paddle alongside another

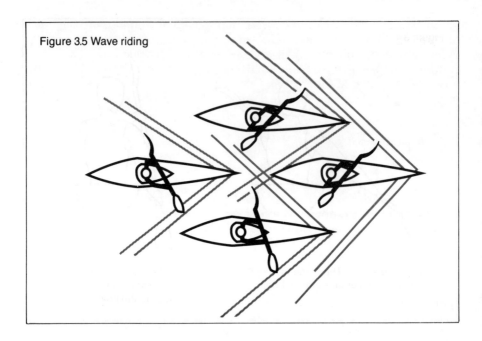

Figure 3.5 Wave riding

canoe leaving just sufficient space between you for your paddle strokes. Drop slightly behind the other canoe so that the wave from its bow lifts the stern of your boat. This means that you are "surfing" on the bow-wave of the other canoe. It saves you a certain amount of energy, making it possible for a group of canoes to travel along in formation, taking it in turns to help one another. (See Figure 3.5.)

Mistakes to be avoided

Wobbling

Although it might sound obvious, keeping the boat steady is more difficult than one thinks. As soon as the boat wobbles it loses speed. The hull is no longer a straight streamlined object, but rather a curved and awkward shape.

Wobbling can be avoided with experience, for as one gets steadier, the less likely it is to occur. It also helps to push on the footrest as one pulls the paddle through the water. As you paddle on the right, push with the right foot. This counteracts the boat's natural tendency to tip over away from the paddle.

Swinging the rudder

If you rest your feet on your rudder pedals, and push on them with every stroke, your rudder will be turned one way then the next continuously. This obviously slows the boat down, as it weaves through the water instead of following a straight course. To prevent this happening, the balls of your feet should rest on the bar of the footrest just below the pedals. When you wish to turn, push on the pedals with your toes. The T-bar rudder controls, now very seldom used except in sprint canoes, have the advantage of a solid footrest so that wiggling from side to side cannot occur.

The K2

Style and *timing* in a K2 are of paramount importance. Two good paddlers who paddle very differently and out of time will be beaten by a couple of synchronised novices using the same style. The paddles must go into the water at the same split second and the emphasis must be the same. Doubles work best if both paddlers use a long, smooth stroke so that neither is pulling harder at certain stages in the stroke.

The paddler in the back has the task of seeing that the stroke and timing are correct. Sometimes this is extremely difficult, for if the front paddler has an unusual, fast or slow stroke, it is the back paddler's task to fit in with it. For this reason, the stroke paddler should always be the one with the smooth, even style, while the back paddler should be the one who is able to adapt and provide the power without ever losing time.

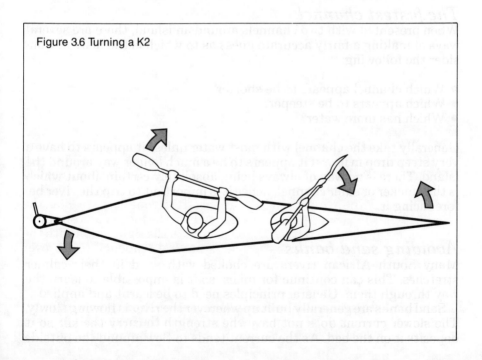

Figure 3.6 Turning a K2

Turning a K2

A very useful combination of strokes to turn a K2 in the river is the bow rudder for the front paddler and the low brace or telemark turn for the back paddler. This makes it possible to turn a 6,5 m-long boat on its axis. It is exceptionally useful in a small tight river such as the Duzi when the nose of the boat is inexorably approaching the bank. The front paddler usually shouts at his partner in a desperate manner to "BRAKE!" He then pulls the nose round with a bow rudder and a head-on with a rock is avoided. (See Figure 3.6.)

River long distance

A paddler who knows what he is doing in a racing K1 or K2 in the river can save himself a significant amount of time and effort. Capsizing, running aground, paddling in the slow water and various other pitfalls can be avoided.

Less experienced paddlers are often impressed by the relative freshness of winners at the end of a race. They do not realise that it is not only a case of fitness but also of saving energy. By avoiding the many pitfalls that slow a boat down in the river, a paddler can minimise the time and effort spent in a race.

The fastest channel

When presented with two channels around an island, there are several ways of making a fairly accurate guess as to which is the fastest. Consider the following:

- Which channel appears to be shorter?
- Which appears to be steeper?
- Which has more water?

Generally take the channel with most water unless it appears to have a very steep drop in it or if it appears to be a much longer way around the island. There is no way of always being absolutely certain about which is the quicker or safer channel, hence it is important to trip the river before racing it.

Avoiding sand banks

Many South African rivers are choked with sand in their calmer stretches. This can continue for miles, so it is impossible to learn the way through them. General principles need to be learnt and applied.

Sand banks are generally built up wherever the river is flowing slowly. The slower current does not have the strength to carry the silt so it deposits it on the bed. As the current tends to flow around the outside of corners, sand banks usually build up on the inside.

A transverse sandbank is usually found across the centre of straight pools as the current flows from the outside of a left-hand corner to the outside of a right-hand corner. In other words, as the current changes from the one outside bank to what has become the other outside bank, so the sand bank swops from the one inside bank to the other.

Here the paddler is faced with the difficult task of deciding when he should swop from one bank to the other. The best way to do this is to look carefully at the surface to see where most current is and to cross there.

Using the current

One should obviously use the current to one's advantage as much as possible. The current flows fastest along the outside of corners and next to the higher bank. The water is also usually deeper next to the higher bank so it is a good thing to look out for. Sometimes, such as on a long or tight turn, it pays to leave this current to cut a corner and save several metres, but if the river is sandy, be careful of the sandbanks lurking beneath the surface.

Resting in rapids

Not only is this a waste of time but it also causes a loss of steerage as the boat travels at the same speed as the water. The rudder is no longer effective and one does not have the power to paddle around objects. Not paddling in rapids is the surest way of wrapping a boat around a rock. If anything one should paddle harder in rapids than on flats and if a rest is really needed it can be taken on the flats after the rapids.

The only exception to this occurs in rough water tripping, usually in polyethylene or slalom canoes. Experienced paddlers will float slowly downstream, using the ferry glide and various effective strokes to manoeuvre about in rapids.

Wild water techniques

The following points apply mainly to the use of rough water kayaks, although many of these strokes are of course used in all designs paddled in rough water.

We are all aware of the incredible uplift a waterski gives when towed at speed behind a speed boat. When putting a moving paddle on still water or a still paddle on moving water, the same principle applies. By angling the blade correctly, it can easily support the weight of a paddler. This dispels the myth of having to have good balance in order to canoe, for the skill lies in the use of the paddle rather than in being able to keep good balance.

The low telemark

This stroke is very similar to the slap support. One rests the back of the paddle-blade on the water and leans on it. This acts like a brake, slowing the boat on that side and hence turning it while remaining very stable.

The high telemark

As the name suggests, this stroke is done with the paddle held high. It should only be used in white water craft which are stable and have no rudders, for the paddle is twisted around putting you in a rather unsteady position.

It is best used to exit a fast current and pull you into an eddy. As you paddle downstream with the current and wish to turn into a still eddy on the side in order to stop, you reach out into the eddy with the blade to pull you in. Your wrists are reversed, i.e. the paddle is held above your head. The one blade is stuck out into the eddy. Lean on the blade and pull yourself towards it. Make sure that you have the blade forward of midway along the boat, otherwise the tail will be pulled towards the eddy and the nose will turn away in the wrong direction.

The slalom paddler uses a high telemark to turn out of a gate. (John Oliver)

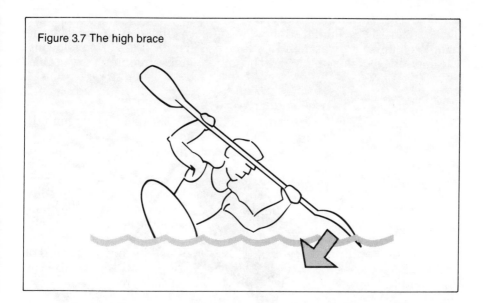

Figure 3.7 The high brace

It is exceptionally important to keep the paddle in front of the body line, for besides being ineffective if done further back, a shoulder is in a vulnerable position for dislocation if your arm is stretched above and behind you. In no stroke should the blade ever be in the water behind you.

It is possible to lean heavily on the blade, which will support your weight even if you lie over on the water. As the boat swings into the still water, you pull the boat over right into the eddy with a draw stroke.

Although the scoop side and not the back of the blade is the side used for this stroke, the grip on the paddle is not altered. In no stroke is the grip by the control hand ever loosened.

The high brace

In large rapids when the boat is easily overbalanced, the slap-support stroke becomes impractical as the paddler is no longer upright but lying on his side, submerged in aerated water. The paddle must then be held high out of the water to be at all effective. The high brace is similar to the Eskimo roll in that the paddle is used to right the boat in much the same way as a roll is performed. It is done in the following way:
- Hold the paddle at shoulder height with the front of the blade facing down on your right-hand side.
- Overbalance to that side until the blade touches the water.
- Lean heavily on the paddle shaft keeping your body down and flick the boat upright with your hips. (Notice how similar this is to the roll.)
- Finally bring your body upright.

The high brace keeps the paddler upright as he rides sideways in a stopper. (Val Adamson)

The draw stroke

Moving sideways is important in controlling a kayak on moving water. The blade is buried deep parallel to the boat and the kayak is pulled towards it. This stroke is often used in the final line-up for a rapid if one finds that one is slightly off-line on the approach. It gives the boat a jump to the left or right.

The sculling brace

In canoeing, the word sculling implies a repeated action with the paddle; in this case the paddle blade is swept continuously backwards and forwards whilst being leant on in order to bring a capsizing canoeist upright.
- Hold the paddle at shoulder height with the front of the blade facing down on your right side and lean over as you did in the high brace.
- In order not to capsize, sweep the blade backwards and forwards on the surface.
- Always keep the leading edge of the blade up so that the blade sweeps along the surface much like a waterski.

Technique 35

The kayak is pulled to the right with a draw stroke in order to line up with a slalom gate. (John Oliver)

Figure 3.8 The draw stroke

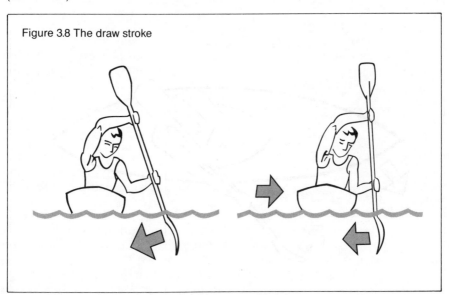

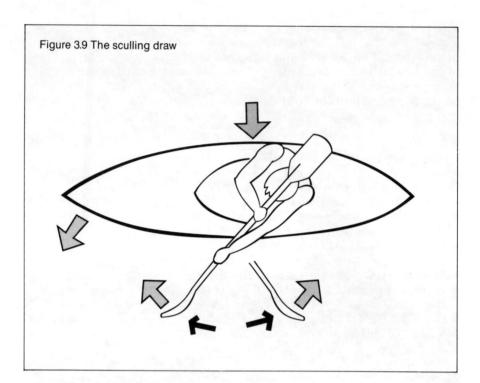

Figure 3.9 The sculling draw

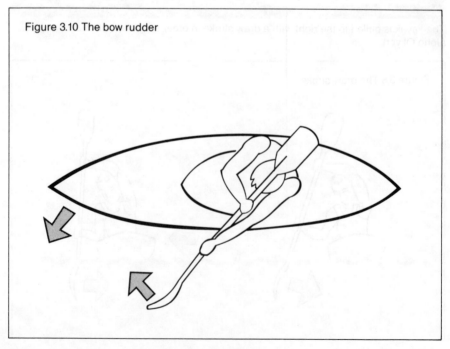

Figure 3.10 The bow rudder

The sculling draw

This is used to pull the boat sideways in one continuous action. The blade is swept backwards and forwards through the water on one side of the boat with the angle of the blade changed continuously so as to keep pulling the boat towards the blade. It is a stroke that is often used on flat water to pull the boat away from the side.

The bow rudder

Possibly the most valuable stroke that there is, the bow rudder can be used in anything from a polo bat to a K2. It is an effective turning stroke that does little to slow the boat down.
- Paddle forward slowly.
- Holding the paddle out in front of you, drop your wrists so that the right-hand blade is facing downwards and slightly forward.
- Put the right blade into the water in line with your knees. Make sure that the paddle is held almost vertically and is in front of you.
- You should feel the pressure of the water on the face of the blade.
- By changing the angle of the blade, you can change the sharpness of the turn.
- Once the turn is complete, force the blade forwards into position for a forward stroke and carry on paddling.

Nanette Rennie uses a bow rudder to turn her kayak without losing speed. (John Oliver)

Breaking into the current: A paddler faces upstream and edges his nose into the current. (John Oliver)

Using the current

Part of the pleasure of white water canoeing is having the power of swiftly flowing water to do the work for you. Always work with the current, whether you are turning, stopping or rolling. Flowing water exerts an incredible force so it is hopeless to work against it.

Breaking in

When setting off in a swiftly flowing river, it is best to face upstream to start with.
- As you set off, paddle towards the current and ease the nose into it. This will spin the boat around and you will be lined up to paddle off downstream.
- Lean away from the flow and brace on the downstream side.
- Always lean away from the current. If you do not, it will push the kayak away from under you.

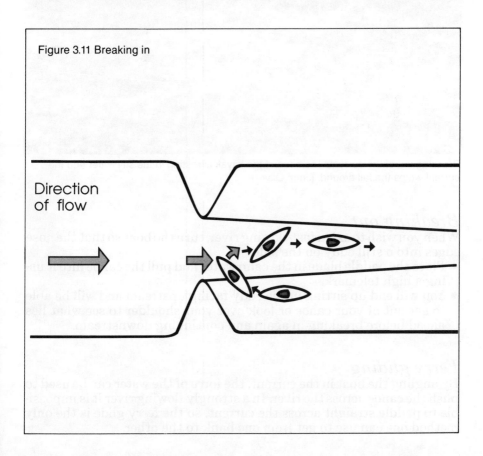

Figure 3.11 Breaking in

Breaking out of the current: The nose of the kayak is resting in the still water and the current whips the tail around. (John Oliver)

Breaking out

When you wish to exit a fast-flowing river, turn the boat so that the nose edges into a still eddy on the side.
- Place the paddle blade in the calm water and pull the canoe into it using a high telemark.
- You will end up sitting in the eddy facing upstream and will be able to get out of your canoe or look over your shoulder to see what lies ahead before breaking in again and continuing downstream.

Ferry gliding

By angling the boat in the current, the force of the water can be used to push the canoe across the river. In a strongly flowing river it is impossible to paddle straight across the current, so the ferry glide is the only method one can use to get from one bank to the other.

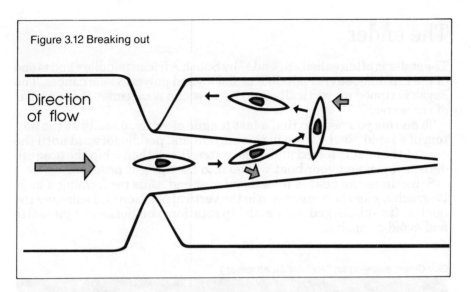

Figure 3.12 Breaking out

- Face upstream against the bank on one side of the river.
- Push the nose out into the current until it is pulled away from the bank.
- Paddle off keeping the boat facing upstream and at an angle of about 25 degrees to the direction of the current.
- As the current pushes on the side of the boat it will push it across to the other bank as long as you keep paddling in order to keep the boat at that angle.

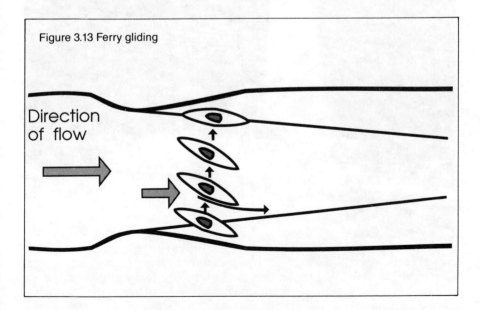

Figure 3.13 Ferry gliding

The ender

The ender is often called an "endo" by South African paddlers and is one of the fun manoeuvres possible in slalom and polyethylene canoes. The kayak is tipped up vertically onto its nose and sometimes shot up clear of the water.

To do this you need to find a fast tongue of water, usually at the bottom of a rapid. Surf a wave in this current and paddle forward until the nose of the boat is forced under the water. It will then whip the nose underneath you and your boat will go into the upright position.

Sometimes the boat is tossed end over end, thus performing a loop. By reaching for the water when in the vertical position and spinning the boat on its submerged nose with hip rotation, you perform a pirouette and avoid a capsize.

Guy Collier enjoying an "endo". (Val Adamson)

Figure 3.14 The ender

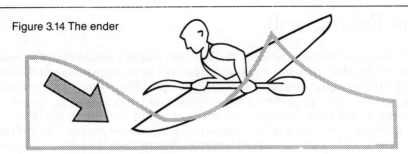

(a) Face upstream and force the nose into the current.

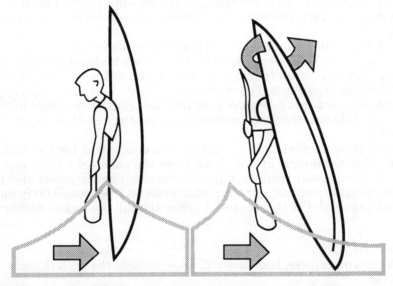

(b) Your boat will be forced upright under you. Reach for the water with your blade and use hip rotation to spin the boat in a pirouette.

(c) You will land upright facing downstream.

The Eskimo roll

For the rough water canoeist, the Eskimo roll is a necessity. At some stage or another you will capsize, and nothing is more rewarding than being able to right yourself and continue paddling. Once you can roll successfully, your confidence will improve and you will be prepared to try things and take chances that you would not have previously.

A paddler who rolls well will sometimes capsize on purpose, to get under a low-level bridge, as part of a manoeuvre in an end-over-end loop, or simply to cool off on a hot day. But the real value of the roll is to right oneself after an accidental capsize. This not only saves time, but can also avoid a nasty swim or a waterladen canoe from breaking on the rocks.

Paddlers with a vague notion of the roll consider it dangerous in the river, thinking that the paddler is likely to knock his head on submerged rocks. This can certainly happen, but it is just as likely to happen to a paddler who capsizes and does not roll. It is quicker to perform the roll than to release a spray cover. A good paddler takes two seconds to right himself. Rolling rather than swimming saves the rest of the body from knocks.

The helmet is obviously a vital item of equipment for the Eskimo roller. When hanging upside down from the capsized canoe, one obviously needs good protection from the rocks. The life-jacket also provides valuable padding, for the paddler can receive several body blows whilst capsized. For this reason, I prefer the full life-jacket designs.

How to roll

1. When you capsize, lean forward, nose towards the deck (Figure 3.15).
2. Pull the paddle from wherever it is to alongside the deck (Figure 3.16).
3. Push the front blade out into the air above the surface of the water.
4. Slap the surface with the front blade to make sure that it is at the right angle to the water, i.e. flat or parallel to the surface.
5. Slide the front blade along the surface until it is at right angles to the boat (Figure 3.17).
6. Flick the boat upright with your hips as you pull down on the paddle (Figure 3.18).
7. Keep your head down for as long as you can. The boat must be upright before you are.
8. You are now set and ready for more action (Figure 3.19).

Some important points

- Rolling is a form of paddle stroke. One does not roll up by pushing on

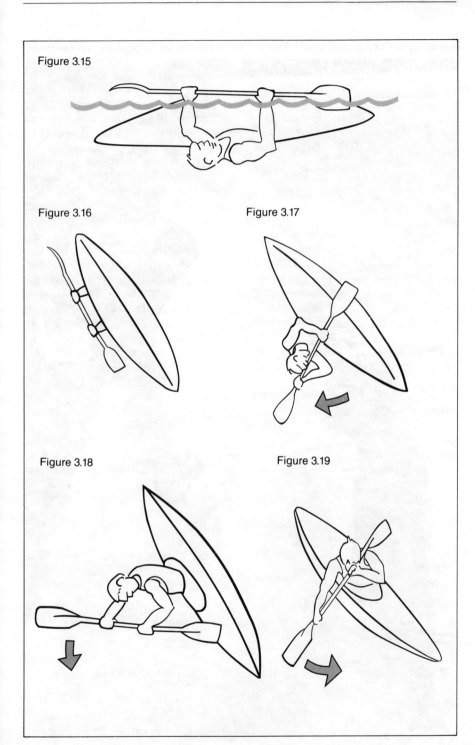

Figure 3.15

Figure 3.16

Figure 3.17

Figure 3.18

Figure 3.19

Practising an Eskimo roll in a pool. This paddler is working on the hip-flick. (Val Adamson)

the bottom, although this is done by non-rollers on some lucky occasions.
- The roll can be performed on either side although most paddlers have a preferred side. It does not matter which side you capsized on.
- It is important to practise rolling upright on both sides for you might not be able to use the side that you favour in certain situations.
- The momentum from the capsize is not used to right oneself; this is a broadly held misconception.

Learning to roll

It is virtually impossible to learn to roll without the guidance of an experienced canoeist. The slightest error in your technique can mean the failure of your roll or a dislocated shoulder, so no matter how strictly you adhere to the textbook, an instructor is needed to correct your slightest flaws.

The roll should be learnt in warm, clear water; a swimming pool is ideal. A wave-ski with a belt is one of the easiest boats to use to learn the roll in, not only because it rolls easily, but also because it does not fill with water if your roll fails and you have to bail out.

Have your knowledgeable helper stand in the water beside you so that he can place your paddle in the right position and help you right yourself if your roll should fail.

Gain confidence in the water by practising capsizing and hanging in the boat. Try to orientate yourself. This is one of the biggest problems in learning to roll for one feels totally lost when hanging upside-down in murky water and tends to bail out before even trying to roll.

Learning the correct body action can be done in the pool by holding onto the side and rotating the hips in the manner illustrated in Figure 3.20.

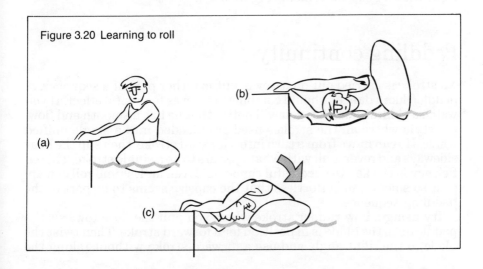

Figure 3.20 Learning to roll

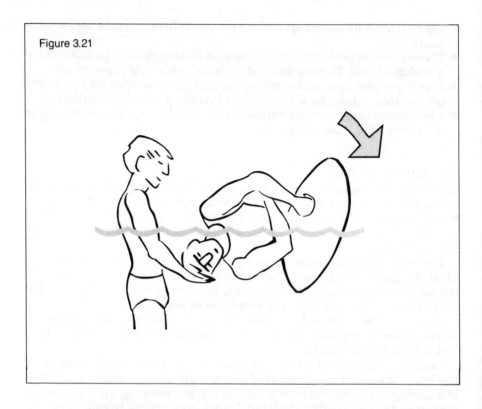

Figure 3.21

Another useful exercise to assist in learning the roll is to have your helper turn you upright by flicking you up with your head. This has the advantage of teaching you to keep your head down and to flick the boat upright with a body movement (Figure 3.21).

Paddling continuity

No stroke is carried out on its own, but is rather part of a sequence. A paddler, like a dancer, should combine his moves for a total effect. If you watch a skillful canoeist, you will notice that he has a smooth and flowing style where all the strokes used are blended into a single unified whole. He can move from a turn into a forward stroke, then slip the boat sideways and reverse all with what appears to be a single stroke. This efficiency is the key to successful canoeing. Even an Eskimo roll can appear so smooth and effortless that the capsize seems to be part of the paddling sequence.

Try using a bow rudder stroke where you pull the nose towards the paddle until the blade is in position for a forward stroke. Then twist the blade to the right angle and use a forward stroke without taking the

A skilled slalomist uses a bow rudder which he will turn into a forward stroke. Such composite strokes are the key to paddling success. (John Oliver)

blade out of the water. You will feel the smoothness and efficiency of this stroke combination.

One mistake that the novice canoeist is inclined to make is to use more strokes than he needs. Every stroke must have a definite purpose and should never be added to a sequence to look good. The main object of racing canoeing is forward motion, so the fewer turning, bracing and other strokes that are made, the better. Every forward stroke lost is time lost.

4 TRAINING

For the canoeist who wants success in competition, a long hard road of watery miles lies ahead. There is no quick and easy formula; the paddler who does best is the paddler who trains best. It takes a couple of years for a talented novice to reach the top, provided that he paddles regularly for an hour or two a day five or six times a week.

There are as many different approaches to training as there are canoeists. Training can be used to develop speed, acceleration, strength and stamina. Different forms of canoeing require different talents so a paddler should try to work out what his strengths and weaknesses are before deciding what type of training best suits him. The type of training done is also determined by the aspect of canoeing in which one plans to participate.

The following list indicates the abilities in order of importance which have to be developed for different aspects of the sport:

Slalom	— acceleration, speed.
Wild water racing	— stamina, speed.
Sprinting	— speed, stamina.
Flat water long distance	— stamina, acceleration.
Rough water long distance	— stamina.

The above points pertain to training only. Different skills also have to be developed in order to perform well in the various canoeing forms. Slalom, for instance, requires boat control and river skill, while flat water long distance requires wave riding and wily tactics.

Different paddlers obviously come into canoeing with different natural abilities. A lean and wiry canoeist usually has a fair amount of stamina but lacks the strength necessary for speed and acceleration. This dictates the type of training he must do. Large, strong paddlers usually do not need to work on strength so concentrate on speed and stamina, but this of course is not always the case. It usually takes a canoeist a full season to find out where his strengths and weaknesses lie. Sometimes it is a good idea to develop one's weaknesses and in other cases it is better to avoid aspects of canoeing which require abilities that you do not have. If you have natural talent in river skills but lack strength, then you would do well to avoid sprints and flat water and concentrate on river racing, whether it be long distance, white water, or slalom.

Most paddlers start by racing long distance, and change to other forms of canoeing once their interest in the sport is aroused. Not all pad-

A relay change over on the Berg River. A K2 hands over to a K1. (Alick Rennie)

"Oordra Plek" on the last day of the Berg River marathon. The late Lance Park avoids portaging by taking the fast option and going through the pipe. (Alick Rennie)

John Edmonds en route to his first Duzi win. (Alick Rennie)

Graeme Pope-Ellis and Tim Cornish en route to winning the 1990 Duzi marathon. (Danie Coetzer)

Quick and deadly; Mark Jamieson sprints up the front of the pack at the start of the 1985 Duzi but breaks his nose on the Commercial Road weir. (Alick Rennie)

Canoes like match-sticks piled on the bank at the Duzi overnight stop. (Danie Coetzer)

Jane and Rory Pennefather shoot down the steps of the Ernie Pearce weir, first obstacle in the Duzi marathon. (John Oliver)

A slalomist pulls his boat into a gate with a bow rudder stroke. (John Oliver)

dlers stick to the aspect of the sport in which they are best, but do that which they enjoy most. Thus flat water geniuses are often seen enjoying rough water canoeing for example, although they would be doing better sprinting.

The secret to performing well lies in starting with your training programme early. It is most enjoyable to race the first event of the season slightly fitter than everyone else. They spend the rest of the year trying to catch up with you and hopefully they never will.

The off-season should be put to good use with weight training and a couple of easy paddling sessions every week. As the season approaches, do less in the way of alternative training such as gym work and running and more paddling. This ensures that you are in good shape for the first race of the season.

It is always a good idea to study the racing calendar before you start your training programme so that you can identify the races that you hope to do well in. You can then plan your training so as to ensure that you will be fit for those events.

Regular training should start about four months before the race which you have given top priority. Every paddler has his own ideas and preferences when it comes to training, so the approach I suggest here must be considered as only one of many possible approaches. General principles apply to training, but how you apply them is your own affair. For example, all weekly programmes should include a long paddle for stamina training and short, hard sprints to develop speed, but how they are ordered depends on what suits you best.

If you are preparing for a long distance marathon, possibly a multi-day event with three to four hours of paddling per day, your programme could look something like this:

Month 1: Paddle three to four times a week (± one hour). This can be relatively slow and comfortable, brushing up on your style.

Month 2: Paddle five times a week. Add variety to your training. Do some longer sessions and some short, faster ones. Interval training can be included. This is a method of doing short, fast sprints repeatedly in order to improve speed and acceleration.

Months 3 and 4: Paddle six times a week. The following weekly programme should get you near to your peak:

Day 1: A medium effort session one hour long with a few random intervals thrown in.
Day 2: A stamina building session of long intervals and high speed cruising — one and a half to two hours.
Day 3: A short, fast session, either 45 minutes of intervals or the same amount of time at full speed followed by a cruise at medium pace for another half hour in order to keep the mileage up.
Day 4: Long hard cruise of one and a half to two hours.

Day 5: Speed work of sprint repetitions.
Day 6: Rest.
Day 7: Race — hard and fast. About two hours.

Such a week would give you nine to 10 hours of paddling. This might seem like too much to the man in the street, but the top paddlers do this and a lot more. Many paddle twice a day. Of course not every one has the time available and one can do well on much less than this, but if you show talent and wish to get to the top, this is the type of training you will have to get used to. Such a training programme does not suit everyone, however, and once you have worked out your interests and abilities, you can work out a programme to suit yourself. It is not the training that builds you up but the rests in between training, so if you are feeling tired from your previous session when you start the next one, you are probably training too often. Even by training every second day, you can become superbly fit as the long rests ensure that you are rested and can push yourself to your maximum at every session.

Paddlers training for the Berg and other long races would scoff at this training schedule. It contains no real long sessions in the order of three hours and more and does not even give the paddler a hint of the pain he is likely to suffer on the Berg. There is a feeling that you have got to hurt in training if you are to get fit. True, hard work improves you, but there is a limit to this. It is possible, in our hot climate, to push oneself to the point of dehydration or hypoglycaemia, especially in training where one does not carry juice. Continuing training under these conditions is foolish. Modern thinking tends towards shorter, faster training.

In 1980 a team of British paddlers came to race the Berg and all four of them finished in the top 10. Their training consisted mainly of one-hour interval sessions, and their longest paddles were trips down the river to learn the way. But they did not win the Berg, and like Comrades marathon runners, it has always appeared as though the paddlers with miles behind them are the ones that come through in the longest races.

Training well also implies living well, in a canoeing sense of course. A perfect day in the life of a perfect canoeist would resemble the following:

5 am: Wake up to a day of hard work, starting with an hour's speed canoeing session.
7 am: A breakfast of fruit, bran cereal, wholewheat toast and honey, and a health drink.
8 am: Fill in training diary, plan further training and weekend river trips. Ask boss for leave to go to a canoe race.
1 pm: Gym session.
2 pm: Eat fat-free lunch of fish or chicken with unpeeled potatoes, vegetables, etc.
5 pm: Hard two-hour canoeing session.
7 pm: Supper of pasta to prepare for the following day's training.
8 pm: Read canoeing magazines.
9 pm: Bedtime.

Such fanaticism does in fact exist and obviously pays off, but I have known paddlers live very different lifestyles and still do very well. Certain sacrifices have to be made, but to adopt this ideal is neither necessary nor desirable. It can lead to staleness and boredom, and most canoeists are in the sport for enjoyment.

Interval training (sprint repetitions)

The human body cannot work at maximum effort continuously. In order to improve fitness it needs alternate periods of work and rest. This also applies to training. To improve speed, numerous short bursts at maximum effort alternated with short rests should be done. This is termed interval training and is especially popular with sprinters, although it is of value to all competitive canoeists.

Numerous interval training programmes exist and it is possible for a paddler to develop a session for himself. New sessions develop continuously, but one principle applies to all of them: hard work improves you. It does not really matter whether you do 30 strokes hard and 30 strokes slowly repeatedly, or one minute hard and one minute of rest a few times, as long as you are working near to your maximum effort on each interval. The following interval sessions are some examples of interval training that can be done; they are not necessarily the best possible, but should give an idea of the type of training interval work is.

Type 1

1. Paddle slowly for about 15 minutes to warm up.
2. Do four one-minute intervals at maximum pace with one to one and a half minutes' rest between each interval.
3. Rest for five minutes.
4. Repeat steps 2 and 3 four times.

This will give you 16 one-minute sprints but the whole session will have taken you almost an hour; quite long enough for an interval session.

Type 2

Pyramid session

1. 10 strokes on, 10 strokes off. Repeat five times.
2. 20 strokes on, 20 strokes off. Repeat four times.
3. 50 strokes on, 50 strokes off. Repeat three times.
4. 100 strokes on, 100 strokes off. Repeat twice.
5. 50 strokes on, 50 strokes off. Repeat three times.
6. 20 strokes on, 20 strokes off. Repeat four times.
7. 10 strokes on, 10 strokes off. Repeat five times.

("Strokes on" means as hard as you can; "strokes off" means slowly in order to get a rest.)

Strokes are counted on one side only; i.e. one stroke is one completed paddle cycle. Count each time the left blade goes into the water. You cover approximately 250 m with 50 strokes. Take a couple of minutes' break between each set. Numerous other types of pyramid sessions can be developed.

Type 3

Intervals according to markers on the bank

If you train on the same stretch of water every day, you might like to choose prominent markers on the bank to indicate your starting and stopping points for each interval rather than count your strokes. Trees, fence posts, jetties and buoys can be used. Try to make each sprint section approximately 250 m long with similar gaps in between. Some might be longer and some shorter, but this helps to prepare you for different length sprints in racing.

Approximately eight intervals can be done before you take a five to ten minute rest. Repeat the set of eight three times.

Type 4

Longer intervals or repetitions can be done, sometimes using race distances of 500 or 1 000 m. The same distance is used repeatedly.

Paddlers usually do six to eight 500 m sprints. If you are trying to develop speed, shorter bursts like eight to twelve 250 m sprints can be done. If stamina is more important then do longer sprints, like 1 000 or 2 000 m four to six times. The latter is particularly useful for wild water racing and the 1 000 m race.

Repetitions of the same length can be varied or combined with pyramids. You could, for example, do three or four 250s, two or three 500s and a couple of 1 000 m sprints all in the same training session.

Never build up your training out of one type of session only. Variety is the best way of coping with the monotony that can set in during training. Avoid making every session a one-hour cruise over the same course as this will lead to staleness and not help you to develop your speed. Try to train on different waters occasionally and alternate speed sessions with long stamina building paddles.

As the race which you have trained for draws near, taper off your training. Don't do any session longer than an hour and a half for the 10 days preceding the race and no really hard sessions in the last five days. Cruise slowly up to three days before and then take a complete break over the last two days. The days immediately prior to a race should be spent "carbo loading" and resting in preparation for the day. In this way you will ensure that you are at your best for the race.

The main principle behind training is hard work interspersed with rest. If you are prepared to push yourself to your limit day after day, month after month, while allowing sufficient recovery time, you will reap the rewards of dedication.

Canoeing in South Africa differs from canoeing in other parts of the world in most ways. Although it is often better and more enjoyable here, it is also often far behind. Our sprinting standard is nowhere near international level and there are numerous reasons for this. Some of the most striking relate to training.

Generally speaking, our paddlers are involved in all aspects of the sport so they do not concentrate on sprint training as much as paddlers from other parts of the world do. Many long, hard training sessions in preparation for marathons slow us down and we do not have the incentive to train or specialise in sprinting. In addition to this sprinting does not enjoy much publicity, a factor which being readmitted to the Olympic Games would no doubt change.

Owing to the lack of canoeing coaches in this country, there is no one to give advice, train and co-ordinate training for paddlers. Money in canoeing goes towards sponsorship and spectacle and consequently there is none available for coaching and training. Rewards from investments in canoeing come from advertising through sponsoring paddlers and events which gain publicity. A company gets a great deal of valuable exposure through sponsoring an event like the Duzi; they would get nothing from donating money towards the payment of coaches.

But if, as we hope, we are poised on the brink of readmission into the world sporting fold, something must be done to raise our standards. Training and coaching might be part of the answer.

Gym work

Most of the work done in a kayak involves maintaining a constant pace over a prolonged period. The movements are relatively easy and smooth; the muscle activity is aerobic and is fuelled by oxygen carried in the blood. Long distance paddlers are endowed with a physical make-up which is particularly suited to this type of exercise. Continuous training in the boat helps to develop such stamina.

However, all paddlers find themselves in situations where they are called upon to apply maximum power to the paddle. This could be to break clear from the bunch at the start of a race, beat the opposition over the line in a sprint finish, accelerate through a stopper, or avoid a nasty drop.

Such activities require anaerobic muscular action. The energy comes from a chemical process which does not require oxygen, although oxygen is used at a later stage. Lactic acid is produced. The paddler eventually feels weak and out of breath as he experiences an oxygen deficit.

He can improve his ability to apply power by presenting his muscles with short bursts of heavy work, either by sprint and interval training in the boat, or weight training in the gym.

When sprinting, for a single forward paddling stroke, you apply a force of 10 to 15 kg to the blade. Think how many times you do this in a paddling session and you will realise what good weight training canoeing really is. But paddling can be complemented by gym training. There is no doubt that using weights increases the strength and therefore canoeing speed.

Gym training is of twofold benefit to the canoeist. Lifting heavy weight results in improved strength, while repetitive lifting of lighter weights or circuit weight training increases the strength and endurance of the muscle.

In the off-season, especially if the weather is bad, gym work provides a comfortable alternative to an icy paddling session. In cold climates, weight training is often the only way of keeping fit in winter. Fortunately most parts of South Africa have all-year canoeing weather, but gym work in the off-season provides a change that helps in fighting off the boredom of flat water training 365 times a year and reduces the risk of muscular injury.

Flexibility

Paddling increases strength but decreases flexibility and a certain amount of flexibility is required for canoeing, especially in the trunk, hips, shoulders and wrists.

Static stretching is best done prior to all weight training and paddling sessions. Stretching should last for about five to ten minutes. This is especially important for rough water canoeing where your muscles are likely to be pulled and contorted into various unusual positions. Most canoeists warm up for white water by paddling up and down a still pool before entering the rapids. Even for flat water, it is best to paddle for a few minutes before the start of a race to loosen up the shoulders and forearms. Stretching on the bank should be included although it goes against macho canoeing etiquette to be seen going through a stretching routine. Sneak off and stretch in secret if you don't wish to be seen as sensible.

Stretching should never be painful. Bouncing and overstretching are counterproductive. A stretch should be held for a count of at least 10 seconds, during which time you apply only mild tension. Never stretch beyond the limits of comfort, and if you have suffered a shoulder injury, seek medical advice before stretching that shoulder.

Some stretching exercises

1. Quadriceps: Stand on one leg. Hold your foot behind you. By pulling on your foot with your upper leg held straight down, your quads will be stretched. (John Oliver)

2. Hamstrings (above): Seated on the floor with one or both legs extended in front of you, stretch towards your toes. The knee must remain straight. (John Oliver)

3. Calf muscles (opposite): Stand away from a wall and lean against it. Press the heel of your foot down. (John Oliver)

4. Achilles tendon: With feet together assume a crouched position. You will feel a pull on the tendons. (John Oliver)

5. Latissimus dorsi (lats): Lean to the side with arms raised above the head. Stretch upwards. (John Oliver)

6. Chest, arms: Clasp your hands behind your back. Press your shoulder blades together. (John Oliver)

7. Shoulders: Cross one arm in front of you. Pull it against your chest. (John Oliver)

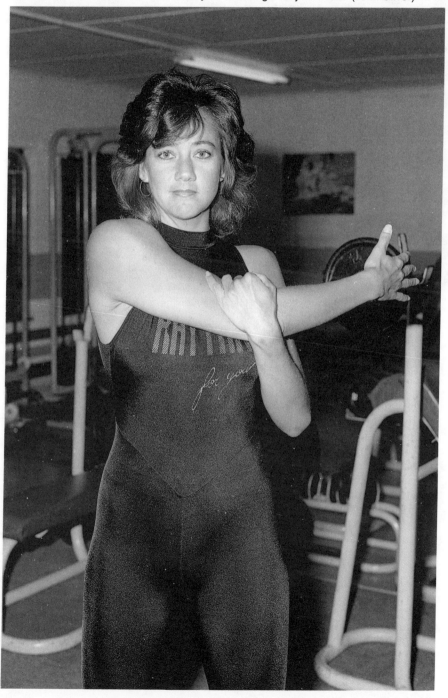

8. Shoulders: Extend arms sideways. Rotate the shoulders. (John Oliver)

Weight training for strength

The general principle behind strengthening a muscle is to overload it. This is done by forcing it to contract against resistance it does not normally encounter. These near maximum contractions stimulate adaptations in the muscle tissue which increase its strength.

A most important factor in weight training is the need to start slowly. Pushing heavy weights too soon can lead to an assortment of debilitating injuries. Start with light weights and increase the overload as your strength improves. Such progressive training is essential in a strength-gaining programme.

One of the principles behind using weights is an attempt to isolate certain muscles or muscle groups and work on them specifically. It is physically impossible to exercise one muscle at a time, but the exercises you use should be aimed at particular muscles, otherwise although you may be improving your strength, it might be in muscles that do not help your canoeing.

If you have not used free weights before, it is best to get advice from an expert as it is possible to injure yourself through poor technique.

Warm up with gentle exercise before starting a session, and once you are warm go through your stretching routine. Only after that are you ready to train with heavy weights.

Although the frequency, duration, number of sets and repetitions of weight training vary amongst canoeists, the norm is supplementary canoe training with weights twice a week for 40 to 60 minutes.

Exercises used in a programme will differ from paddler to paddler, but the important basic principles remain the same. The exercises must be specific to paddling and overload the muscles that are used in canoeing. The Duzi canoeist who needs to run with his canoe on his shoulder should include leg work, hence the inclusion of leg building exercises. A typical example of a weight training programme for canoeing would include the following.

1. Leg extensions. (John Oliver)

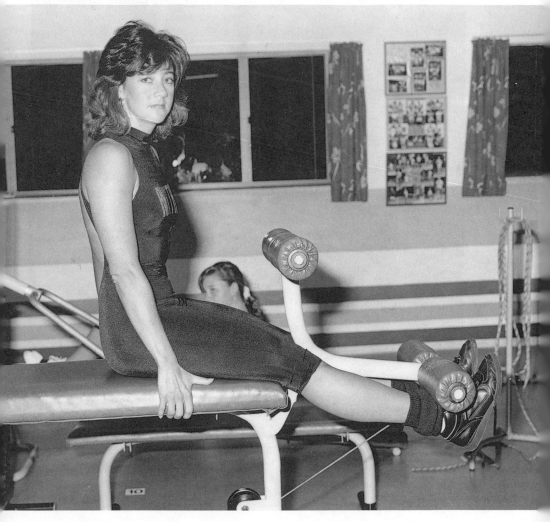

2. Leg curls. (John Oliver)

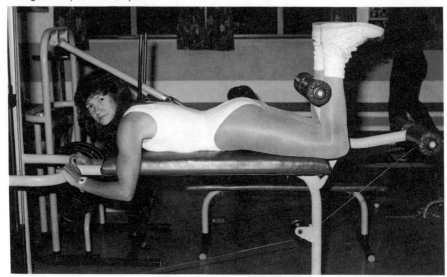

3. Dumb-bell pullover: Place upper back on bench. Hold dumb-bell directly above you, then lower it behind you and bring it back up. (John Oliver)

4. Bench press: Lie on back and hold bar directly above you. Bend elbows until bar almost reaches chest. Restraighten arms. (John Oliver)

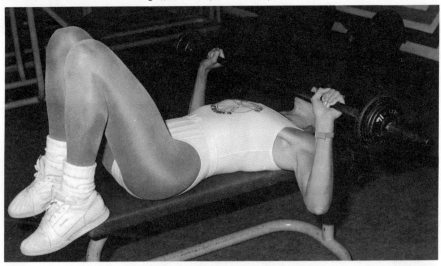

5. Seated rowing: Using row machine, pull handle towards you repeatedly with both hands. (John Oliver)

6. Canoe machine paddling: Adopt seated canoeing position. Pull with one hand as you release with the other, similar to the canoeing action. (John Oliver)

7. Side lateral raises: Holding dumb-bells in front of you, raise the arms sideways to shoulder height. (John Oliver)

8. Bent over flies: Place your head on a high bench in order to support your lower back. Raise the dumb-bells to shoulder height. (John Oliver)

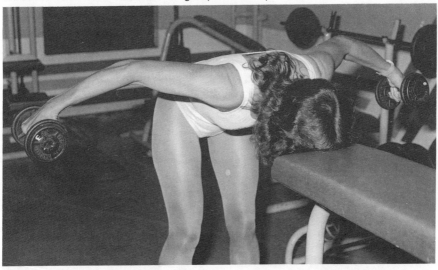

9. Hammer curl: Hold dumb-bells at sides with palms facing inwards. Raise one dumb-bell as you lower the other. (John Oliver)

10. Triceps kick back: Lean over and rest your weight on a bench. With a dumb-bell in your hand hold the top part of your arm parallel, then straighten your elbow. (John Oliver)

11. Bent leg sit-ups and knee roll (below and opposite): These two exercises are done together. First lie on an inclined bench and do sit-ups with knees bent until your stomach burns, then swing around and lie on your back. Raise your legs and trunk at the same time then lie back again. Repeat until your stomach burns and change back to sit-ups. Do three sets of each. (John Oliver)

If you do not have access to a gym, there are several exercises that you can do with a minimum of equipment in order to improve your strength. These include the following.

Exercise	Muscle used
1. Chin-ups (using normal paddle grip)	lats
2. Chin-ups (using reverse grip)	biceps/triceps
3. Press-ups (increase the weight on your arms by raising your feet on a bench).	chest/triceps
4. Diagonal sit-ups.	stomach
5. Dips (between parallel bars).	chest/triceps

Recommended training programmes

Although training is very specific and each paddler needs to work out his own training programme, it is interesting to know what some successful paddlers are doing in order to turn in their exceptional performances. The following programmes are recommended and used by three of the top paddlers in South Africa, each of whom is outstanding in his particular field of the sport.

Duzi training programme
Graeme Pope-Ellis

No paddler in South Africa has been as successful in his particular field of canoeing as Graeme Pope-Ellis has in the Duzi. For the two decades in which he has dominated the race, he has adapted and altered his training continuously so that he now has a programme that is more tried and tested than any in the country. It is not merely a theory but a practical success, and the result of 20 years of research.

There are basically three types of competitors:
1. The person who wants to get by with the least amount of training, whether to finish just within the cut-off time or to finish mid-field.
2. The person who really tries his best (or thinks he is trying his best) but is never really happy with his performance and finishes in the mid to upper part of the field.
3. The person who wants to win.

Bearing the above in mind, I think we should have two training programmes, but remember that the harder you train, the more you enjoy the race.

A flexible muscle trained correctly over a substantial period of time is incredibly strong and durable and can take an awful amount of punishment. You must start slowly, both paddling and running, and gradually build up *fitness* and *strength*. You must get fit enough to get fitter in order to reach peak fitness. (You cannot build a double-storey house on single-storey foundations. A good farmer does not plant good seed in a badly prepared seedbed where the plant cannot get a good root system.) In short, you will be a better athlete if you start slowly and train correctly.

Programme A is designed for the paddler who just wants to finish the Duzi. Programme B is for the paddler who wants to win.

Training programme A

With the Duzi in the latter part of January, you must start training in July/August. If you have run the Comrades, the cross-country season or paddled the Berg River Marathon, and thus kept a little fitness through winter, you need only start in August/September.

For the first two to four weeks do an easy run twice a week of 4 to 6 km and an easy paddle of ±30 minutes two to three times a week on alternate days to your runs.

For the next six to eight weeks merely increase your training time by ±10 minutes on each session and do one running time trial and one canoeing time trial a week.

If you have been able to train like this so far (five days a week for six to eight weeks), take a break of about a week and then go on again as before for another six to eight weeks. This should take you to November.

From November to the end of December, try and get in at least three paddles of about three hours and three runs of about one and a quarter hours. Otherwise keep training as before.

Start tapering down in the last three weeks before the race and rest altogether for the two to three days preceding it.

It is a good idea to do a little gym work from September to November, not only to strengthen your canoeing and running muscles, but also the muscles around them in order to avoid injury. Always spend a little time stretching, particularly when doing gym work. Try and run on rough and uneven terrain to strengthen ankles, knees, thighs and back. There are only 5 km of tar running in the Duzi.

Try and join your club at every opportunity you get to go over the course of the Duzi, either with or without your canoe. It is good training and gives you a change of scenery to prevent you from becoming stale.

After the race try to paddle and run as you did in your first two weeks of training.

Training programme B

I try and avoid ever having more than a 72-hour rest during a training period and train five to six days a week. I break my training into two distinct phases: one continuous period of six to eight weeks, followed by a rest for about four days, then a second six to eight week stint of training.

Background training

With the present Duzi rules (which do change from time to time) one should train about 30 to 40 percent running and 60 to 70 percent paddling.

Gym training: I start with fairly heavy weights in June/July, with 10 to 15 repetitions, and continue with them until September. I then do circuit training up to within three or four weeks of the Duzi to bring me up to peak and help with my speed.

I believe in working only my upper body in the gym; my legs are worked by running hills. However, if a paddler is injury prone or has weak legs, I would recommend leg work in the gym. It is worth bearing in mind that gym work is a supplement and not a substitute to the training programme.

If you are weak at paddling, your Duzi training should start with the Berg River marathon (training begins in February/March). If you are weak at running, do the cross country season in winter. If you need both then do both, but if you are training to do well in the Duzi then running the Comrades is a NO NO NO!

By 15 October my background training is over and I am ready to do my 12 hard weeks of specific Duzi training. This, as mentioned before, is a six-week training stage followed by a three to four-day break then another six weeks of really hard training.

Running and canoeing

The following sessions are included in every week of canoeing training:
- Intervals
- Pyramids
- Canoeing time trial
- An easy session
- One very hard session of ± 1 hour 20 minutes

I run in the mornings and paddle in the evenings — one or two days hard, then one day fairly easy. On weekends I race or go over the course of the Duzi, either with or without the canoe.

Running with the canoe should only start in about October once or twice a week, gradually increasing to three or four times a week in December. In January drop down to two or three times a week. I get in three hard days of about three to four hours of non-stop training three times from 15 November to 31 December. They are spaced five to ten days apart, giving me time to recover between sessions. This is the time that one feels pain in the chest as arms and legs are strong enough at this stage to see one through.

Any training done under one hour is speed training, and any over an hour is done as stamina training.

A typical training week from October to December

Monday
a.m. Run hill or pyramids ±15 minutes
p.m. Canoeing pyramids
Tuesday
a.m. Fairly easy paddle
p.m. Run time trial 5 to 8 km
Wednesday
a.m. Run with boat, 45 minutes
p.m. Canoeing intervals
Thursday
a.m. Run hills or intervals ±45 minutes
p.m. Canoe time trial

Friday
a.m. Easy run with boat 30 minutes
p.m. Hard 90-minute paddle
Saturday and Sunday
I race on either Saturday or Sunday; on the other day I do a fairly easy run and paddle one after the other; 30 per cent running and 70 per cent paddling in time. The total training time should be about two hours at 60 per cent effort.

I treat all races as training, and therefore do not rest for a day or two before races. I only start tapering down three weeks before the Duzi. I train hard for 45 minutes every second day and go fairly hard for an hour on the intervening days, then rest completely two to three days before the Duzi.

Training for sprints
Peter Peacock

Peter Peacock dominated sprint canoeing in the 1970s and remained unbeaten in 1 000 and 10 000 m races in South Africa in the latter part of the decade. He was most successful in singles racing, but also turned in some remarkable K2 performances with Robbie Stewart and Tony Scott. His domination of sprint racing was so overwhelming that few paddlers remember his five Duzi wins with Pope-Ellis. The latter performances dim somewhat when compared with his sprinting successes.

The following sprint training programme was used by Peter Peacock to attain his exceptionally high competitive level.

Training for sprints can be broken into three phases per year:

Phase 1: Basic conditioning and strengthening (eight months)
During this phase I include:
- Long distance races.
- A general weight training programme to increase strength.
- Running, especially if the Duzi is an intermediate goal.

The effort of the paddling is increased before races I consider important.

Phase 2: Transitional period (four to eight weeks)
The training during this period depends on how much fitness and strength I have acquired in the previous phase. The quality (i.e. speed) of training is increased and distance is reduced. Sessions range from 60 to 90 minutes and comprise even-paced, fast paddling including surges of speed (i.e. fartlek training) from

four to ten minutes long. The speed during surges is not so fast as to be exhausting and a reasonably fast pace is maintained between surges.

I intersperse hard sessions with easier slower paddles and check up on technique. If the training is done correctly, one notices a gradual improvement of fitness during this phase. Some low-key interval training can be introduced towards the end of this phase.

I introduced specific strengthening exercises into my weight programme.

Phase 3: The final build-up (six to eight weeks)

The quality training done now is tailored to develop weak points. Stamina-oriented paddlers should work at speed and very fast paddlers should work on stamina at speed.

Intervals, repetitions, time trials and starts are all included in my programme as the quest for speed begins in earnest.

(a) Interval sessions

I do two to three sets of intervals in one training session. A set consists of eight to ten one-minute bursts of speed with a two to three-minute rest between bursts. After each set, I take a five-minute recovery rest.

Note: Paddling between intervals can be fairly fast with slightly slower bursts (stamina-oriented), or slow between intervals with fast bursts (speed-oriented).

Effort on intervals should be uniform throughout the session. Fading or slowing at the end of each set or after three or four intervals indicates that the interval is being done too fast.

(b) Pyramid intervals

Pyramid intervals consist of sprints that get longer and then shorter each time. The first one is 15 seconds, the second 30, the third 60, etc. A full set would look like this: 15−30−60−90−60−30−15. I do three to four sets with a short break after each sprint and paddle comfortably and continuously between each set.

(c) Repetitions

Repetitions are done over a fixed distance from a standing start. The period between repetitions is long enough to ensure that I recover completely and can do each interval at maximum speed.

The repetitions I do are usually half a minute, one minute (250 m), or two minutes (500 m) long. Long repetitions improve stamina at speed, short repetitions improve speed.

Speed on repetitions should be constant. Any variation of more than three seconds over 500 m towards the end of a session indicates that the first repetitions were done too fast.

(d) Starts

I do between four and ten starts at the end of some sessions. Initially start with the boat moving slowly (the pull is easier) and

as technique improves progress to standing starts.
(e) Time trials
Time trials over 1 000 m are done about three times in the last six weeks at the beginning of short training sessions.
(f) Fast, even-paced paddles from 50 to 75 minutes.

My schedule during phase 3 includes all the above training methods. The final mix of these sessions should depend on the individual's abilities. A very fast paddler with limited stamina will do a stamina-oriented programme (more continuous paddles with slower intervals and faster recovery paddles, and fewer repetitions). A slower paddler will weight his programme towards developing speed by doing fast sprints with slow paddling in between and will do many repetitions.

The races in the early part of the season are used as training and provide the chance to experiment with race tactics.

Note:
- When training at high intensities, the rest periods between intervals are as important as the intervals themselves.
- Monitor your body weight. Any sudden weight loss means you must reduce your training.
- An increased pulse rate also means you are overdoing it and must slow down on training.
- Taper off with four days of light training before a regatta.

A typical training week early in phase 3

Monday	Three sets of six one-minute intervals (two to three minutes rest in between).
Tuesday	Hard and fast evenly paced paddle (60 to 75 minutes).
Wednesday	One 1 000 m at maximum, three 500 m, four one-minute repetitions.
Thursday	Three sets of six one-minute sprints.
Friday	Eight one-minute repetitions. Pace of intervals is kept constant.
Saturday	Rest.
Sunday	Race. If there is no race I do an even paddle or long pyramids, e.g. 20 minutes fast, then 10 minutes fast, then five minutes fast.

A typical training week late in phase 3.

Monday	Fast, even-paced paddle, or medium pace if I have raced on Sunday.
Tuesday	Three sets of six one-minute sprints.
Wednesday	Six 500 m sprints.
Thursday	Pyramid-type intervals.
Friday	Eight one-minute sprints.

Saturday Rest.
Sunday Race.

(Note the change in emphasis from stamina at speed related training in the first part of phase 3 to shorter speed work in the later stages.)

Weight training

Initially I use a general strengthening programme but soon adopt a specific weight training programme. This develops the muscles required for paddling.

The following exercises are some of the ones I use in order to build strength for sprinting.
1. Sit-ups.
2. Chin-ups.
3. Dips on parallel bars.
4. Bench press.
5. Military press.
6. Trunk raising backward.
7. Dumb-bell curls.
8. Upright rowing.
9. Bent over rowing.
10. Pulley rowing.
11. Press behind neck.
12. Push-ups.

Long distance training

Mark Perrow

Mark Perrow is one of the more successful all-round paddlers in the country at present. He has dominated the South African canoeing scene in white water racing, sprinting and long distance, and is also a competent rough water tripper. The following is his description of the training he used to win the 1990 Berg River marathon.

My training for the Berg started six weeks before the marathon. I had just come out of the sprint season, which helped develop my speed tremendously. Without sprinting, one does not have a chance of winning the Berg. Speed has become a necessity with the large number of competitors and the need to sprint for the wave and at the finish of stages. The sprint season is about six weeks long, so it provides an excellent speed base for the Berg.

Five weeks before the Berg

I was in hospital during this week from a stomach bug, but it should have been my distance week. I had planned to paddle between one and four hours per day with one rest day, and paddle one 10 km time trial during the week.

Four weeks before the Berg

Monday Rest.
Tuesday Two hours. Four of us trained in a group, each pulling for 1 km. We covered each kilometre in 4,05 to 4,23 minutes. We did the last 10 km in 44 minutes.
Wednesday One hour's paddling in a group. Felt very tired.
Thursday Rest. Travelling to Cape Town from Johannesburg.
Friday Train Bridge to Bridgetown on the Berg. Slow. Getting to know the river.
Saturday SA K1 Championships. Hermon to Gouda on the Berg River. 32 km. Very fast pace, two hours.
Sunday Misverstand to Kersiefontein, 65 km. Hard and fast with short rests.

Three weeks before the Berg

Monday Zonquasdrift to Bridgetown, 45 km.
Tuesday Six 250 m sprints with 15 seconds rest between each sprint. Repeated three times, i.e. 18 250 m sprints in the session.
Wednesday One hour, 18 km. Flat water training in a group.
Thursday Pyramid training.
Two 250 m; two 500 m; two 1 000 m; two 500 m; two 250 m at 80 per cent effort.
Friday Rest.
Saturday Misverstand Dam. Two hours, 30 km, including two 2 000 m sprints at 100 per cent effort.
Sunday Gouda to Bridgetown, looking at river.

Two weeks before the Berg

Monday Sandrift to Soutkloof, 20 km. One hour, eight 500 m intervals.
Tuesday Three sets of six 250 m intervals.
Wednesday Gouda to Bridgetown 32 km. Looking at river.
Thursday Pyramid training.
Two 250 m; two 500 m; two 1 000 m; two 500 m; two 250 m at 80 per cent effort.
Friday Rest.
Saturday Springbok trial race. Four hours fast, 52 km.
Sunday Two hours, 30 km, relatively easy.

One week before the race

Monday Zonquasdrift to Bridgetown, 45 km, three hours. Looking over river.

Tuesday Paarl to Hermon with 15 250 m intervals.
Wednesday Skooltjie to Hermon with intervals. Two hours, 25 km.
Thursday Gouda to Bridgetown, 32 km.
Friday Rest.
Saturday Paarl relay, 45 minutes flat out. Skooltjie to Hermon, 30 km trip.
Sunday 32 km light training.

Race week

Monday Rest.
Tuesday Rest.
Wednesday Berg. Day 1.
Thursday Berg. Day 2.
Friday Berg. Day 3.
Saturday Berg. Day 4.
Sunday Rest.

I feel that a certain number of very long training sessions are necessary because it is important to put your body through at least two days of what the Berg is going to be like. It is also necessary to test your seat over long periods of time to make sure you are comfortable enough to take several hours of it.

Although training sessions may appear to be long and monotonous, boredom is overcome by group training and the inclusion of intervals in long sessions.

Most of my training sessions are done with four or more other paddlers. This makes training more interesting and enjoyable as well as providing high intensity training. Training in groups is also beneficial because it teaches one about tactical paddling.

Training on the river is important on the Berg, for it not only familiarises you with the route and its many channels, but it also helps you adapt to the "swirlies". These are small eddies formed by the flowing water which affect the path of the paddle through the water. If you are not used to swirlies, your wrists swell up and this can lead to tendonitis.

5 SPRINTS

Sprint canoeing is a test of flat water speed. The canoeist develops his ability with one purpose in mind; to go as fast as possible in a straight line on flat water. To do this the paddler needs a certain amount of strength, and an exceptionally efficient style. He must, of course, also be superbly fit, for he cannot rely on river skills and route knowledge to give him an advantage over other competitors.

Senior men compete over three standard distances: 500, 1 000 and 10 000 m. The shortest of these take less than two minutes, and the longest roughly 45 minutes. There are some long distance races that are marginally shorter than the 10 000 m sprint, differing only in the canoeing conditions, so it is the conditions as much as the distances that make canoe races sprint or long distance events. Women and juniors race over 500, 1 000 and 3 000 or 5 000 m.

The sprint course consists of nine buoyed lanes 1 000 m long. Each paddler in the 500 and 1 000 m event has a lane to himself, thus only nine paddlers can compete at a time. Heats are held to select the top nine paddlers to compete in the finals. Each lane is sufficiently broad so that no paddler can ride another paddler's wave.

Sprint races are never held in harsh or adverse conditions, for these would affect the paddler's style and efficiency. No paddler is allowed to have an advantage over another such as a sheltered lane while others are windswept. For this reason sprints are held on calm inland waters so that conditions are the same for every paddler.

The 500 m

The 500 m race, the shortest of the sprint events, is done at top speed just about all the way. The paddler starts as fast as he can and holds on to his maximum speed as far as is possible for the entire race. The tactics and effort required for it are very similar to those of the 800 m track athletics event. Both races test the combination of speed and stamina in an athlete.

There are many approaches to paddling the 500; this is just one of them: Take off as hard as you can and keep up the maximum effort for approximately 30 seconds. By now you have got your canoe to its maximum speed. Ease off slightly at this stage; the momentum you have built up helps to keep you cruising at a high pace. Keep paddling just off maximum effort for about the next minute, which should carry you to about 30 seconds from the finish. If you are very fit, you should be able to go at maximum pace again until you get there. The fitter you are, the sooner you can start sprinting for the line.

If raced properly, the 500 should leave you feeling totally drained. As you are racing in a lane with no canoes near you, you do not slow at any stage to ride on a wave. You are therefore using as much energy as you can as efficiently as possible, and this should leave you none at the end. Being fit, you will recover quickly and be ready for the next race within a few minutes!

The 1000 m

Often considered the hardest sprint distance, the 1 000 favours the fit rather than the strong paddler. It has gained "classic" status in canoeing circles as it used to be the standard Olympic distance. Now all three senior distances, (500, 1 000 and 10 000 m) are included in the Olympics.

Like the 500, the 1 000 is also raced in a straight line, each paddler having a buoyed lane to himself. Start this race with almost as much effort as the 500, but keep a little in reserve even at the start. Once the boat is cruising near to its top speed, relax a little and settle into a pace which you feel you can hold until the finish. A good natural style, plenty of stamina and fitness and a healthy work ethic now come into play. You

A 500 metre K1 race. Speed is all that matters. (Val Adamson)

Ngumeni hill portage on the Duzi second day. (Danie Coetzer)

Tim Biggs does an ender in a competition slalom kayak. (Val Adamson)

A controlled pirouette by Alick Rennie. (Jerome Truran)

Surfing on one of the lower waves in Island rapid. (Alick Rennie)

Mark Perrow surfing on the Umzimkulu. (John Oliver)

Island rapid on the Umgeni. When in flood it becomes Durban's Colorado. This paddler heads for a massive stopper. (Alick Rennie)

He is unable to penetrate it and stops dead . . . (Alick Rennie)

. . . before being sucked back and thrown end over end. (Alick Rennie)

K2s form a hard working group in this 10 000 metre event. (Val Adamson)

must be prepared to hurt yourself, pushing harder than is comfortable. Your high speed cruise should last until you are nearing the finish, then pick up the pace as much as you can over the final 100 m.

The 10 000 m

This 10 km race resembles a long distance event. Wave riding is an important technique, for groups of canoes form and share the work. On every corner or whenever a paddler is badly positioned, the pace picks up and paddlers are shaken off the wave. In this way the leading group becomes smaller so that there are fewer to reckon with at the finish.

The final 1 000 m straight is the most important part of the race, for paddlers move up in order to have a good sprint for the line. Those with a good "kick" are the ones that win, for they can sprint ahead over the last couple of metres.

Successful sprinting

A good style is the single most important factor in successful sprinting. All the power in the world is of no use if it is not being utilised correctly. Also important is fitness, for one cannot rely on rapids, portages or others' accidents to help one to the front of the field. No paddler has an advantage over another, so to win you must be fittest.

The sprint season in South Africa is usually held in April and May. This fits in well with canoeing in the summer rainfall region for paddlers have background fitness from months of river racing. As the sprint season draws near, paddlers intensify their training, changing from long, slower sessions to short, fast, speed work. Some will paddle twice a day, doing speed work in the mornings and stamina training in the evenings. (See Chapter 4 for various training sessions.)

The start is very important in sprinting. Half a boat length gained in the first 50 m is sufficient to give a paddler an unassailable lead in a 500 or 1 000 m race. It therefore makes good sense to practise your starts. The general idea is to pull a couple of short, hard strokes before lengthening as this gets you moving quickest. One paddle blade should be in the water when the starter's gun goes. Your arm should be bent slightly so that the strongest part of a stroke will be exercised as you take off. Try various starting techniques against other paddlers and with a stopwatch to work out how you can take off fastest.

When lining up for the start, make sure that you are up on the line and stationary. Avoid moving in front of the line before the start as the starter will call you back, and while you are reversing he could start the race. Your initial stroke will then be stopping the boat rather than moving it forward and you will lose a couple of metres on your opposition.

Taper off your training in the week prior to the major sprint regatta of the season (see Chapter 4). In this way you will ensure that you are on top form for the event.

Always **warm up** before your race. Most paddlers like to warm up in the 20 minutes prior to their event. They will get on the water and paddle easily for five minutes before doing a few short sprints and a five-minute medium-pace paddle. They then paddle straight to the start.

Others warm up an hour before the start. They get on the water and paddle gently for 15 minutes, then sprint as hard as possible for 250 or 500 m. They then get out of the canoe, their muscles and joints loosened but not tired, and rest for 40 minutes before their race.

Stretching exercises should also be done on the bank, for sprinting, unlike long distance, does not give you time to loosen up while you are paddling (see Chapter 4).

Besides the pleasure of feeling exceptionally fit, an advantage of sprinting not always considered by non-sprinters is the good it does for a paddler's development in other aspects of canoeing. A good sprinter is usually a good white water paddler, slalomist and long distance racer, for he has the speed and strength needed in all situations. Sprinting is also a challenge, it is character building and develops your mental and physical abilities. The long-term effects of continual training show in later life.

6 WILD WATER RACING

Wild water racing is a test of speed through rough water. The competitor comes to the starting line alone. He faces a course approximately 5 km long, consisting of continuous rapids of grade 3 difficulty.

Both fitness and skill are required in order to negotiate the course as quickly as possible. Numerous training trips down the course beforehand ensure that the paddler knows the fastest route through every rapid.

Competitors are set off by the starter at one-minute intervals and the one to cover the course in the fastest time is the winner.

With the combined velocity of the river and the boat, things happen fast. One has to be extremely alert and fit in order to keep going at full speed for the 20 or so minutes that the course takes. A wrong stroke or line-up for a rapid can cost a position as paddlers complete the course within split seconds of each other.

A team race is also held, where three boats race down the course together. The time of the slowest boat is taken as the team's time, so it is the object of the team to help the slowest paddler to speed up his run. This is done by making it easy for him to ride on the other boats' waves on the few flat sections and by staying out of his way in the rapids.

The Bushman's River at Estcourt in Natal is the home of white water and slalom canoeing in South Africa. There are several reasons for this, not the least being the Bushman's suitability for white water racing. It is a fast-flowing river with continuous medium-sized rapids. These test the paddler's canoe control without being so large that one is concerned with survival rather than speed. Water levels are guaranteed with releases available from Wagondrift Dam, so the river is never low for competition. But most important, Ralph and Cheryl George, who live in Estcourt, make an enthusiastic and hard-working team, organising events from the negotiations for water to time-keeping and the importing of overseas paddlers. Under their care, white water racing has flourished.

Other rivers in Natal and the eastern Transvaal also provide suitable white water courses, but access to the best sections and the possibility of low water has limited their use. The Umzimkulu and Umkomaas in Natal and the Lowveld Crocodile in the eastern Transvaal are used on occasion.

The wild water course usually takes 20 to 30 minutes to complete. This means that the pace is fast, so paddlers try to develop high speed cruising from sprint-type training. The successful wild water racer needs to combine speed with boat control and river reading. He must always take the fastest line, so is faced with the dilemma of sacrificing forward speed to increase boat control.

Two diverse types of wild water racers therefore develop. There are the slalom-type paddlers who always take good, fast lines, but lack the speed of flat water paddlers. They are often able to beat the faster paddlers by saving time and energy through successful route choosing. The sprinters tear down the course at great speed, often losing their lines and paddling through the slow water rather than in the current. Obviously the best white water racers are those that combine boat control with speed most successfully.

Controlling a fast, rudderless boat in rapids is no easy task. The slightest side current or eddy can throw the boat off line and even lead to it spinning around to face the wrong way. This is the type of time wasting that the paddler has to guard against.

The racing line

There is only one right way through a rapid when racing and that is the fastest route possible. An experienced paddler would be able to mark this line on the surface of the water with a pen (if it wasn't that the ink runs!) It is so narrow and well defined in his mind that it operates much like a rail. His object is to stay on the rail, for if he goes off it, he gets into upstream-flowing eddies and slow, turbulent water.

It takes experience to find the racing line, but within a season of river

Neil Evans concentrates hard on keeping to the racing line. (Val Adamson)

and wild water racing, a paddler is able to find it quite successfully. In deep, open rapids it is generally found as close to the waves in the current as one can possibly get without the waves breaking on the deck. As soon as the boat starts to bounce, it loses speed. Always avoid stoppers and take the tongue down drops and through waves. Look for a smooth ride without ever getting out of the current.

Always keep a look out for faster lines down rapids than the ones you are using. See if there are any corners you can cut, or rapids that are negotiable in a faster way. Paddle down the wild water course with experienced canoeists and see which lines they use. Perhaps they can save you some time.

Knowing the racing line is one thing; staying on it is another. A white water boat with no rudder and a straight rocker line (a straight rocker increases speed but sacrifices turning ability) can be a beast to steer. It is therefore important to line up properly at the top of a rapid and hold the racing line at all times. Do not let the boat drift so much as a centimetre off its route, as it becomes almost impossible to get back on line again. It is therefore better to slow down marginally in rapids and speed up again on the flats.

Pacing

A white water race is just long enough to test your stamina and just short enough to test your speed. You cannot take the course at maximum speed for you will run out of energy half-way through. Much like the 1 000 m sprint, there needs to be a balance between speed and energy conservation. If you take off too fast, you will not only run out of steam, but be too tired to paddle through the rapids on the right line. Besides wasting time you could mess it up thoroughly and end up capsizing. If you are out of breath you will not be able to roll.

Thus it is important to pace yourself. Start off hard but use the first kilometre to settle down and get good lines. Keep up a hard and steady pace for the first half of the course. By this time you will be tiring and need to dig down deep for that extra bit of energy to go even harder. The last flat should be tackled with all you've got, for the split second saved could make the difference between winning and losing.

Warming up

A problem common to wild water racers is sore, stiff forearms soon after the start. This can be totally debilitating, even making holding the paddle difficult. It is the result of not warming up properly and then taking off fast.

To warm up, exercises on the bank can be done, but most important is

Three white water paddlers race down the course in a team event. (Val Adamson)

a paddle on the river before the start. I like to paddle over the entire length of the course before my timed run, but if this is not possible, I will do part of it or get into the river upstream and paddle down to the start. This gets you wet, relaxes you and gets you in tune with controlling the boat in rapids. Your arms warm up and no muscles are likely to tighten up in the race. Do not race down the river in your warm-up run before the start. Just paddling in rapids will have you working sufficiently to loosen you up.

Unlike long distance in this country, white water has not adapted to South African conditions. It is modelled and raced on international lines with courses being short and always in the form of timed runs. This makes it easier for local paddlers to compare their talents with overseas canoeists, but in a country where the emphasis is on mass participation and pleasure, the fitness and finesse of white water canoeing does not appeal to the sporting masses as much as the socially enjoyable long distance races. The sport has therefore remained relatively small and is practised mainly by a select band of white water enthusiasts. This gives it an élitist atmosphere which is inclined to frighten the beginner off and consequently keep the sport small. In the seventies it was raced very much like long distance with mass starts for white-water boats down longer sections of rough water. This form of racing was more popular and should perhaps be reintroduced for some non-championship events. It might boost the interest in true time-trial white water racing.

Tim Whitfield powers his way through a gate. (John Oliver)

7 SLALOM

Canoe and kayak slalom, like ski slalom, has the paddler weaving to and fro from gate to gate down the course. What makes canoe slalom interesting is its inclusion of rough water. It is a test of speed and precision, gauging the paddler's ability to control his boat in rough rapids. It differs from white water racing in that the slalomist is led into the rougher and more difficult parts of the rapid by the course, while the white water racer avoids such trouble spots.

The competitive slalomist is perhaps the most competent of rough water paddlers, as he is able to control his boat superbly in the most difficult conditions. It is this slalom training and ability that has made canoeists such as Jerome Truran, Alick Rennie, Rowan Sampson and Sean Rice pioneers in rough water canoeing.

The slalom course consists of approximately 25 gates hung over the river which must be negotiated in a certain sequence. A rough section of water about 500 m long is chosen where paddlers need rough water skills in order to perform well. Like white water racing, the paddlers race against the clock, being set off by the starter one at a time.

Nanette Rennie lines up for gate 5. (Val Adamson)

A gate consists of two poles approximately 2 m apart. They are strung from wires above the river and the paddler must pass between the poles to negotiate the gate successfully. If he touches a pole, five seconds is added to his time. If he deliberately pushes it around him, or misses a gate completely, he is penalised by 50 seconds. Gates are watched by judges who record your score.

Besides negotiating gates in numerical order, paddlers must pass through them in a designated direction. Downstream gates consist of two green and white poles while upstream gates have red and white poles. Negotiating them in the wrong direction also adds 50 seconds to your time.

The course is designed to give the paddler several options on how to negotiate the route. The difficult way should obviously be the quickest, and the paddler is credited for using this route. The run is planned from the bank first, then from the boat in the period set aside for practice. Each competitor gets two runs down the course, the faster of the two being the one that counts for the final score.

Team events are also held in slalom. A team consists of three competitors, who are set off at the same time. They all amass penalties which are added to the time of the slowest paddler to give the final score. Here paddlers have to ensure that they do not crowd each other and force each other into poles, thereby incurring penalties.

An upstream gate is placed in an eddy between two tongues of fast flowing water. A slalomist should never be made to work against the current. (John Oliver)

Alick Rennie shows the balance and power that has made him one of the best slalomists in the country. (Val Adamson)

More important than speed in slalom racing is the ability to control the boat in rough water with great precision. One uses the current to the best advantage, crossing from one gate to the next as fast as possible. Familiarity with your kayak and a knowledge of how it will react in certain situations ensure accurate boat control. Using the correct stroke at the right time helps towards a fast clear run. The ability to stay upright in awkward situations is vitally important, for if you capsize and fail to roll you are disqualified. A successful roll does not add penalties provided that the paddler still negotiates all gates correctly, but in a sport where split seconds count, a paddler cannot hope to win if he wastes time in rolling. A good roll takes two to three seconds.

Slalom is a small sport in this country, practised by a band of skilled enthusiasts. It is held almost exclusively on the Bushman's River in Natal around the town of Estcourt, where the river offers several suitable sites with easy access. Several good spots in other parts of the country are also used, but to a much lesser extent.

Despite the intense demands of slalom, this aspect of canoeing gives paddlers the chance to socialise and watch much of the event themselves, for a paddler is only on the water for a few minutes at a time. The rests between runs can often be as enjoyable as the runs themselves.

Slalom training
Alick Rennie

Alick Rennie is a Springbok slalomist with international experience in Europe, Britain and the USA. He has won the South African slalom championships on numerous occasions, and is admired particularly for his planned and thinking approach to slalom training. Few paddlers have approached training in a more scientific and methodical way, and not just slalomists but all canoeists would do well to approach their training in a similar way.

First I believe that one must enjoy training and find it interesting. At the start of the season and early in a competitive career there is usually no problem with this as improvements are noticeable and satisfying. Towards the end of the season and often in the final build-up to an event where improvements are more subtle, problems arise. To combat boredom and lack of interest, I believe in a system of targeted training. Before each session I like to define exactly what I am hoping to achieve in that session. This targeting then extends further to define the aims for each week of training and ultimately each season's competition. This requires planning and self-analysis to pinpoint one's weaknesses; invariably these are the facets of training that are least enjoyable. It unfortunately follows that these less enjoyable areas need to have most time spent on them.

Physical preparation for sports events is a topic that has been covered in great detail in numerous texts, and the serious slalom paddler would do well to consult some of these, especially *Lore of Running* by Tim Noakes and *Essentials of Exercise Physiology* by Lorry Shove. They explain in detail the concept of three energy systems and the training methods best suited to conditioning each system. Basically the three systems are:
- *The ATP-CP system:* this provides "burst energy" for up to about 20 seconds and is effectively the energy stored in the muscles.
- *The anaerobic or lactic acid system* comes into play next for a maximum of two to three minutes.
- *The aerobic system* provides energy for long periods of time.

As a slalom event is usually three to four minutes long and requires numerous accelerations, the first two energy systems are the most important. However, the aerobic system cannot be ignored as this provides the core on which to build the other two. In a long event, the paddler draws on this system. A mistake I have made in the past is not to achieve a high enough level of aerobic fitness before working in the anaerobic systems.

Preparation for competitive slalom requires a great deal of technique training as well as physical preparation. A paddler with sound technique but who is a bit out of condition will invariably do better than a fitter competitor with poor technique.

How do I train to improve my technique? This is the question that I am most often asked by paddlers. The first thing is to set up gates on flat water and practise the basic moves on them. I like a minimum of five strung out in a pattern similar to that one would find in a race. Preferably they should be adjustable in height and on sliding bearers so that their positions can easily be changed. Five gates set out like this can provide most gate sequences.

To perfect technique then requires patience and self-analysis. Start slowly with a selected sequence, a break out say, and establish exactly what strokes are used where. Once this is done, gradually increase the pace. This early technique work can be combined with aerobic conditioning and the moves repeated in "continuous loops" through the gates. Once the stroke sequence is second nature at a fast aerobic pace, it is time to start doing it at sprint speeds. To work on the lactic system first, 10 to 15 gate sequences should be paddled involving the specific stroke sequence that is being targeted. These 10 to 15 gate courses are then paddled flat out as "intervals". During the rest periods don't just sit there and pant; carefully analyse your own and your training partner's performance. A good practice if two or three of you are training together is to watch the paddler's helmet as he comes through the course. Where it stops in turns, gates, etc., there is a problem. Ideally the paddler should move the whole time. The stopwatch should be used for these speed sessions and every effort should be made to bring times continuously down.

So far no mention of rough water gates! Once a sound technique has been developed on flat water it is time to get into moving and rough water. Here the current differentials will effectively speed up the gate sequences. It goes without saying that at this stage you must be completely at home in your boat in rough water. This is achieved by tripping and playing in the early season and not using gates. Such tripping can be combined with stamina training. As the season progresses the emphasis becomes more and more on quality rough water paddling interposed with flat water sessions to polish technique and also to provide a rest from the physical strain of rough water paddling.

I have found weight training to be an important supplement to training in the boat and use a three to four month build-up of compound circuit training. This system enables heavier weights to be used than in pure circuit training and develops strength not obtainable in the boat. I work up to a maximum lift of about 120 per cent of body weight. In the last six to eight weeks before the prime competition period I phase out this compound circuit work with heavier weights and replace it with pure high speed high repetitive circuit work.

A typical year's plan would be as follows:

Phase 1: Winter and spring

Technique — Flat water gates on longer courses.
Physical — Long paddles and compound circuit training building up strength.

Alternate a harder physically oriented session with a lighter session concentrating on technique.

Phase 2: Spring and early summer

Technique — Flat water and rough water gates. Rough water trips with playing and boat confidence work. Start to do gates at high speed (10 to 15 gate sessions).
Physical — Alternate longer paddles with high speed work and medium to long interval work (30 seconds to three minutes).
Weights   — Compound circuit weights coming up to maximum weight.

Phase 3: Final phase (mid- and late summer during the slalom season)

Technique — Very high speed short three to four gate courses. Alternate rough and flat water interspersed with full-length courses. Also practise memorising full-length courses.
Physical — High speed short intervals, starts, etc. with a few longer courses and longer paddles to maintain aerobic condition.
Weights   — Circuits with light weights at high speed.

The following weekly training details are from my 1984 training log when I was a full-time student. Obviously since starting work things have altered somewhat! I no longer do two-hour trips on Wednesday mornings for example, but aim to get as near as possible to what I consider was my best training plan.

Phase 1: August

Monday   Evening — weights.
Tuesday   Evening — one-hour paddle with gates at 60 to 70 per cent effort, developing technique.
Wednesday Evening — one-hour paddle in K1 or WW boat.

Thursday Morning — circuit training.
Evening — one-hour paddle working on technique.
Friday Rest.
Saturday Morning — weights.
Evening — long sequences of gates.
Sunday Long paddle and run.

Phase 2: October/November

Monday Morning — paddle on gates.
Evening — weights.
Tuesday Midday run, 30 minutes.
Evening — gates for one hour; 15 to 18 gate courses timed.
Wednesday Morning — rough water trip; about two hours.
Evening — weights.
Thursday Gates, rough or flat water.
Friday Rest.
Saturday Morning — weights.
Evening — rough water gates.
Sunday Competition or competition simulation.

Phase 3: Training in the final week

Monday Morning — light run, 20 to 30 minutes.
Midday — circuits, weights.
Evening — rough water gates.
Tuesday Morning — flat water gates, technique.
Evening — rough water gates.
Wednesday Morning — run, 20 to 30 minutes.
Midday — circuit weights.
Evening — long paddle in WW boat.
Thursday Morning — flat water gates.
Evening — rough water gates, a hard session.
Friday Easy rough water gate work; a "rest" session.
Saturday Rest — travel to race; perhaps do a light paddle on medium water with easy gates.
Sunday Race.

Mark Perrow and Neil Evans; perfect timing despite the rough water of Black Rock rapid on the Bushman's River. (Val Adamson)

8 LONG DISTANCE RACING

Many rough water enthusiasts are surprised at the interest shown by beginners in racing canoeing. They consider it inappropriate that inexperienced paddlers should start canoeing in the most unstable of boats. It takes them weeks to learn to balance and a full year before they are relatively competent. By contrast they could start canoeing in more stable rough water canoes and once they have mastered these move on to the less stable K1s and K2s.

This would obviously be a sensible approach, but it has certain drawbacks. Firstly it requires the purchase of two canoes; a stable model to learn in and a racing craft once you are competent. Secondly, even for the inexperienced, racing provides interest and company. One meets many other canoeists in racing, learns from their mistakes, has someone to follow down unknown rivers and generally gets initiated into the canoeing world. Canoeing in a suitable beginner's canoe but missing the fun of a race can be a lonely experience. Many paddlers realise that they are starting canoeing in the wrong design of boat, but it keeps the sport alive for them.

Races like the Duzi marathon present an irresistible challenge to aspiring canoeists. Many do not want to become good canoeists or even experienced canoeists, but simply competent enough to finish the race.

Doug Retief and Marlene Louwenstein negotiate Albert Falls weir. (Val Adamson)

For this reason they will buy a racing canoe, become sufficiently skilled to qualify and then hopefully make it to Durban.

A remarkable number of canoeists who originally started canoeing for long distance racing branch out into other aspects of the sport. A race like the Duzi introduces them to the delights of rough water canoeing as well as the possibilities of using the canoe for sight-seeing, tripping and camping.

Many of the country's top sprinters, slalomists and wild water racers were also initiated into canoeing through long distance racing and then branched out as their interests dictated.

Nevertheless, long distance racing remains the most popular form of canoeing in South Africa, for it is suited to all people interested in the sport. The newcomer can cope with the relatively easy sections of river used and it provides spectator interest, making it possible to find willing seconds. It also gives paddlers the opportunity of meeting many other canoeists, sharing their experiences, and learning from them.

Long distance racing includes races on rivers and dams ranging from 10 km courses taking less than an hour to four-day 200 km events such as the Berg River marathon. Extremely rough water is often included like the grade 4 rapids on the Umkomaas. Long distance races can resemble obstacle courses where paddlers shoot massive weirs and roll under low-level bridges. They also give canoeists an exciting outdoor adventure, and all in all provide an activity which becomes so engrossing that one finds oneself involved in a whole canoeing sub-culture.

The following races are some of the ones that rear the fanatical canoeing breed.

The Duzi marathon

Pietermaritzburg nestles in the Umsinduzi Valley approximately 130 km by river from Durban. The usually quiet and uneventful town becomes a hive of activity and excitement every January, when over a thousand canoeists gather to take part in what must be one of the greatest canoeing spectacles in the world.

For several months prior to the race interest runs high. Races throughout the country are geared towards the marathon, with paddlers being required to finish four of them in order to qualify for the Duzi. Canoeists deliberate on which canoe designs to use and how to train. They spend weekend after weekend learning the route, even deciding on which side of a rock to go in order to save a few vital seconds.

As 1 500 canoeists set off from the start on Camp's Drift Canal, one wonders how so many canoes will fit into a river barely broad enough for two canoes abreast. The field is divided up into several different starting batches which eases the congestion, but even the paths on the portages clog with canoes. This is not the only hazard: weirs, rapids, dehydration and sunstroke also threaten the canoeists.

A bow rudder stroke being used to good effect in a K1. (Val Adamson)

Although named the Duzi marathon, the race also includes the Umgeni River which the Duzi joins 50 km from Pietermaritzburg. Both rivers flow through the scenic Valley of a Thousand Hills, appreciated for its beauty by canoeists during training trips.

The river route from Pietermaritzburg to Durban is not entirely canoeable, with various gorges, waterfalls and meanders cut out by paddlers. This entails several portages, some up to 10 km long. A good Duzi canoeist must therefore also be a good runner. It is essentially a race for the biathlete. The talents of the most successful Duzi canoeists bear testimony to this. Both Graeme Pope-Ellis and John Edmonds have represented Natal for canoeing and cross-country running. There are few runners who can run with these Duzi greats and even fewer canoeists who can paddle with them. But it takes more than natural ability to win the Duzi.

Pope-Ellis has adopted a healthy, self-disciplined lifestyle, to which his success must also be attributed. He trains twice a day, usually running in the mornings and paddling in the afternoons, easing off slightly in the winter months. His diet is healthily balanced and gym work is included in his training programme. The weekends in the three months preceding the race are spent scouting the route. Such rigour has earned him Duzi domination for the past 20 years and has possibly given him exceptional health advantages. One just has to think of Wally Hayward's performances in the Comrades marathon in his late seventies and eighties to appreciate the advantages of life-long exercise.

Thorough preparation and a truly professional approach are also needed if one hopes to do well in the Duzi. Pope-Ellis does not reach his fitness peak several weeks before the race or a month after. His equipment does not let him down, his seconds know what he needs and when to give it to him and previous river trips help ensure that he makes no mistakes. One does not have a fluke win in the Duzi. It requires the precision of a ballet dancer and the preparation of a military manoeuvre.

The aspiring Duzi canoeist obviously does not have winning in mind when entering the race for the first time, but by preparing for the race in a professional manner, he can improve his time and have a more enjoyable three days.

The choice of canoe

The Duzi is raced alternately as a singles or doubles race. In a singles year, doubles may enter but are not eligible for prizes, and vice versa. All the top canoeists compete in the major class.

Most novice paddlers prefer to race in a K2. Not only is this considered easier than K1 canoeing, but it also offers the advantage of companionship. However, a K2 does present certain difficulties. Doubles are generally more stable than singles, but being longer and heavier are less manoeuvrable. They are inclined to get stuck and damaged in shallow water and can be broken in half all too easily. In canoeing, things do go wrong: rudders can break and boats can leak or capsize. In a single one can only blame oneself; two tired paddlers are inclined to blame each other. Having a partner can become a case of having someone to fight with.

On the other hand, singles too have their disadvantages. They are difficult to carry alone and can make the race a lonely experience. They are also slower than K2s and most lack stability. But a model suited to the paddler can be an absolute pleasure to use. They are far more manoeuvrable than K2s and more forgiving in the rapids.

I would suggest that canoeists try both K1s and K2s before making a decision as to what to paddle in the race. Get to know the characteristics of each type to avoid a choice you might regret. If you prepare correctly, you will be equally competent in singles and doubles. It is then a good idea to race in the major class and feel more a part of things.

Be conservative in your choice of design. Do not use a boat in which you feel unstable. A fast canoe is not fast for you if you keep falling out of it or have to brace and wobble your way along instead of pulling on the paddle. It is interesting to note how often the Natal and SA championship races held on the river have been won in slower, stable designs.

Rather have a boat that is too heavy than too light, weight means strength. There is not much point in having a light canoe that holes easily and subsequently carries several kilograms of water. If you are going for a gold medal you will need a boat on the limit weight, otherwise a 12 to 14 kg single or a 20 to 25 kg double will serve you best. The limit weight for a single is 12 kg and for a double 18 kg.

Expensive materials such as kevlar and carbon fibre are not absolutely necessary in the construction of a Duzi canoe. They have become prohibitively expensive, and much of their light weight advantage is lost with the limit weight ruling. Kevlar is exceptionally durable, however, so one does feel better about scraping over rocks in a kevlar boat, but many of the top paddlers no longer use it. Fibreglass builds a boat strong enough for Pope-Ellis and you.

Other equipment

Most of the equipment needed has been dealt with in Chapter 1, but certain specific items relate directly to this marathon.

Spray covers should be light and waterproof. They must also be quick to slip on and off as eight to ten entrances and exits are made in a day. It is therefore best to keep running or paddling for relatively long sections and not to keep chopping and changing.

Paddles 2 cm shorter than those used for flat water canoeing are often better in the Duzi as they ease the strain of pulling in shallow water where the resistance on the paddle is markedly increased.

Drinking bottles in the heat of the Duzi are a necessity. The twin soft bottled Sippers and Trippers carry as much as 3 litres. Although heavy when full, they more than compensate for their weight. If you have seconds who can top you up en route, carry 1 to 2 litres and change your bottle when possible. Approximately 1 litre per hour is usually suffi-

Graeme Pope-Ellis shoots Dip Tank weir at the end of day two in the 1985 Duzi. The weir lies deep beneath the waters of Inanda Dam. (Alick Rennie)

cient. Drinking too much is an unlikely problem to have in the 35 °C heat of the Duzi Valley.

The importance of drinking during the race cannot be overemphasised. Make sure that your drinking bottle cannot let you down and start drinking before the race. By slowly sipping away from the time you wake up in the morning, you will ensure that you do not start suffering from dehydration early in the race.

Shoulder pads protect one from excessive chafing and bruising in the long portages. All that is really needed is a thin layer of closed cell rubber stitched into each shoulder of a T-shirt. Large American football-type pads are unnecessary. With time the skin on your shoulders hardens and you can do away with pads altogether. Plaster stuck straight onto the shoulder also provides good protection.

Duzi training *(see also Chapter 4, page 50)*

Training for the Duzi, although similar to training for any other race, becomes more complex in that running has to be included in the programme. Ideally a competent canoeist needs five months to prepare for the race. Three months of background paddling and running provide a good base for the final two months of intensive hard work.

September, October, November

Run 8 to 10 km three to four times per week. Get into the habit of doing this in the early mornings as the evenings are needed for paddling. Pick up the speed of your runs as you feel ready to. Do not rush it and ease off if aches and pains develop. Introduce variety into your running programme, with one fast run, possibly an 8 km time trial, and one long run (15 to 20 km) per week.

The first day of the Duzi involves about 18 km of running so one obviously has to be fit to manage this carrying a boat. To make the running part of the race tolerable, you should be doing approximately 50 km of running a week.

Once you are running fit, perhaps after one month, try running with your canoe. At first it will feel very uncomfortable and awkward, but practice will improve this. If you cannot get a single to feel comfortable, try using a harness. These harnesses take some getting used to, but with time can be mastered. Resting on both shoulders, they distribute the boat's weight evenly. The canoe is inclined to bounce so a smooth running style needs to be developed. Fitting and removing the harness wastes a little time and few of the top canoeists still use them, but anyone who doubts their advantages should see Danny Biggs in full cry whilst using one.

In November and December you should be running five times a week:
- One long run
- One fast run
- Two sessions portaging the canoe
- One slow, easy run.

Taper off your training about two weeks before the race to make sure that you do not start tired.

Canoeing training for the Duzi is similar to any other type of canoeing training. Five to six paddling sessions a week is ideal. It is important to combine canoeing with running to get used to paddling with shoulders sore from portaging. If you are running twice a week with a canoe, make one of those sessions a run/paddle combination. Practise getting in and out as fast as you can. Use a spray cover and see how fast you can put it on and take it off. Know how you are going to put your paddle into your boat; make sure that you and your partner are not "sword fighting" when jamming your paddles into the cockpit.

Get sufficient practice paddling on the river. It does not necessarily have to be on the Duzi race course, as long as you are developing river skills. You should try and get out there at least once a week for two to three months before the race. The weekly races provide the ideal opportunity to brush up on your river paddling.

The race
The start is the tensest part of the race, but once you are on your way, you should settle down and start enjoying yourself. The entire first day is paddled on the Duzi, and includes several long portages. It is the shortest of the three days in terms of distance but the longest in terms of physical strain.

Duzi legend, Andre Hawarden, gets under way after a portage. (Alick Rennie)

Marlene Loewenstein portages Commercial Road weir soon after the start of the Duzi marathon. (Alick Rennie)

On the second day paddlers tackle the Umgeni confluence section, which provides some of the largest rapids on the river. Portages are few and short in comparison with the first day and the good paddlers start to pick their way through the field, making up the time they lost on the "runners" during the first day.

Despite the notorious Burma Road portage on the final day, this stage also favours the better paddlers. Inanda Dam and the Umgeni Blue Lagoon provide a large amount of flat water, and the good rough water canoeist can also paddle around Burma Road, saving energy and gaining time. All in all it is a race which has come to favour the canoeist over the runner to a large degree, which should obviously be the case in a canoe race.

To many paddlers, the Duzi is the only canoe race that warrants the time and effort spent in training. Its carnival atmosphere and spirit of camaraderie make it a thrilling race to compete in. Unlike so many canoe races which lack publicity and public involvement, the Duzi enjoys much public interest and in this respect can be compared with the Berg River in the western Cape and the Sella Descent in Spain.

The Umkomaas

The Umkomaas marathon is the roughest long distance canoe race in the world. When the river is flooding, a canoe is borne along at over 25 km an hour. A continuous line of massive brown waves stretches ahead of you, crashing down on your deck and spray cover and occasionally engulfing you as you hold your breath and feel the full force of this mighty river.

The 120 km route tests paddlers to the full. While negotiating one rapid, one contemplates the next. The pools between the rapids are too short and fast flowing to allow the canoeist the chance to change sides and cross the river; it must be half accomplished in the previous rapid. Such a fast river is very unforgiving. One wrong move and you can end up in a section of monstrous waves and stoppers. Even a 7 m long K2 is easily gobbled up in the holes of a flooding river.

But the sheer speed and volume of the Umkomaas make it one of the most exciting rivers that is regularly paddled in the country. One becomes airborne as one flies off the top of the roller-coaster-type waves. The miles disappear as one is carried inexorably downstream.

The Umkomaas marathon is held in late February or early March each year when the river is likely to be reasonably full. Of course a full river can never be guaranteed, but even a low one offers excitement. There are paddlers — although many might not admit it — who actually prefer a lower level. It is a lot safer and tends to favour the fit rather than the brave. In any case, much of the pleasure of this race is in the scenery, and a lower river gives the less experienced paddler the chance to see this spectacularly mountainous valley.

I emphasise the effect a difference in level makes because it is so extreme that it feels like paddling on two different rivers. One of the things that makes rapids so difficult to grade in this country is the effect of these massive fluctuations in water level. A low Umkomaas is a relatively safe river, but the distance makes it hard going. A full one is safer than it feels, but those who have fallen out in it will vouch for its dangers. Paddlers with some experience, if they have competed in the Duzi for instance, should not be put off by the numerous horror stories. Sample the pleasures of a low to medium Umkomaas first and don't stop there; one of the easier sections such as from Number 8 Rapid to St Josephine's Bridge will give you a true taste of the delights which this river holds when it is full. As your experience and confidence grow you will start to enjoy some of the best canoeing available anywhere.

How to paddle in the Umkomaas

Paddling in a low Umkomaas is much like paddling in any other river used in long distance racing, but a full river requires its own technique. It is similar to that used in wild water racing in that one tries to stay in the fast current, but the big waves which come crashing down on the paddler and his spray cover are avoided as much as is possible. When you are spending five or six hours out on the water, it is vitally important to keep your boat dry. Few of the more competitive paddlers stop during the day, so any water that enters the boat has to be carried to the finish or pumped out; both tiring and time-consuming activities. If your boat is taking in water too fast, a stop to empty it out is necessary.

Despite the river being 50-odd metres wide, there is usually only one correct racing line downstream: as close to the waves as possible without them breaking on top of you. This is not always possible, but the big holes in particular should be avoided. Not only do they stop you and waste valuable time, but they also suck you very deep, filling your boat with water or capsizing you. Umkomaas canoeists are often seen desperately craning their necks in search of holes that lie camouflaged in the frothy brown water.

Holes are formed in the downstream side of large sub-surface rocks. They are largest where the river is flowing fast, which usually occurs on the outsides of corners. It is therefore best to stick to the inside of the main current on bends with your neck craned in search of holes, and move out if any should appear in your line.

At some stage during the race all paddlers have the unpleasant experience of being gobbled up in a hole. When you see this is about to happen, paddle like crazy. You must hit it with as much momentum as possible in order to carry yourself through. Use the slap-support stroke once you are in it in order to remain upright, and start paddling as hard as you can on surfacing from its murky depths. Speed is the best way to deal with the upstream pull of a large hole.

Another hazard one faces in the Umkomaas marathon is extreme exhaustion, especially if one is seated in the front cockpit of a K2. The large waves give one a continual beating on the chest. Your energy is sapped away, with every wave eventually feeling like a body-blow from a heavyweight boxer. Added to this is the extreme distance each day, often in excess of four hours' paddling. A 2 litre drinking bottle per paddler is a necessity, and if you are not totally obsessed with position and time, a short picnic stop for chocolate or sandwiches is advisable. Corn syrup and chocolate bars can be taped inside the boat in some easily accessible place so that they can be removed and eaten without having to stop and get out.

A tired paddler is inclined to make far more mistakes than a fresh one, so it is important to conserve energy to avoid reaching the point of exhaustion. If the paddler in the front of a K2 is wearing out, it is a good idea to swop cockpits and share the exhaustion.

The Umkomaas marathon route
Owing to problems of access dependent upon the condition of roads in the valley, the marathon does not always include the same sections of river. Sometimes the start is at the Hella-hella Bridge, thus incorporating the notoriously rough Number 1 to 8 rapids section. In other years,

paddlers set off from St Josephine's Bridge on the Richmond/Ixopo road. The finish is situated at the mouth of the river, Goodenough's Weir or Mpompomani Rapid. The overnight stop of this two-day race has also been shifted accordingly, dependent on access and in an attempt to keep both days similar in length.

River sections
I will discuss all sections of the river used in the race in order to make sure that there is a brief guide to all parts of the race irrespective of any changes to the route.

Hella-hella to Number 8 Rapid
This is the most awesome and exhilarating section ever used in the race. There are eight numbered rapids in the 14 km section, but many of the unnumbered ones are just as big and difficult. Try and paddle this section under the guidance of an experienced canoeist who knows the river. All the rapids are shootable by a competent paddler, but look carefully at Number 5 and 6 (actually one rapid), also known as Robbie's Special. It contains some strategically placed rocks and waves which demand a positive and quick-thinking approach.

If you survive this section in a full river you can rightly call yourself a skilled canoeist, especially if using a K1 or K2, knowing that you have paddled the biggest rapids ever regularly negotiated by such narrow racing craft.

Number 8 to St Josephine's Bridge
This is one of the calmer sections of the race, and you are now provided with some relief from the wild upper rapids. The river still presents continuous rapids with large waves, but the horror of the grade 4 monsters is over — for a short while at any rate. You now have the chance to really enjoy the river. Your canoe is carried along at tremendous speed, there are few rocks in the main current or near the surface and you are able to belt along without worrying about holes, capsizes or wrapping. You now know why you took up this sport and feel a tremendous sympathy for non-canoeists.

St Josephine's Bridge to Riverside
With luck the euphoria lasts, for some mean rapids lurk unexpectedly on this otherwise easy section. You can only rely on your river skills to get you through them, for they lie hidden and confused in even the most experienced paddler's mind. After St Josephine's Bridge, fold after identical fold of mountain appears, and it is best to try and remember where the big rapids are by measuring the time it takes to reach them from the bridge. This of course implies prior knowledge of the river, but if you cannot acquaint yourself with the river before the race, you will have to follow the paddler in front of you. Do not simply follow him blindly; use both his good and bad moves to decide upon your own. Your

common sense and experience should be equal to his.

St Josephine's Bridge is often used as the start of the race. This certainly makes the race much easier, missing out the Hella-hella section, and gives paddlers a relatively easy first day. The overnight stop is then positioned about 15 km above Mpompomani Rapid. This does, however, make a very long day, with top K2s taking four hours or more to complete the stage. A mid-fielder should bank on five to six hours.

The first real landmark passed on this day is St Elmo's Farm. It is situated on the right bank about one and a half hours after the start. The road to the farm is visible and offers one of the few easy escape routes from the valley for paddlers in trouble. A handful of spectators are usually only too happy to transport you back to civilisation. It is an ideal spot for an overnight stop and appears likely to be used as one more often in the future.

From St Elmo's to Riverside Store (another site sometimes used as an overnight stop) the rapids become trickier, but the river generally maintains its earlier benign nature.

Riverside Store is easily missed, but is of little importance unless you have a broken canoe and are looking for a way out of the valley. Always ask the local people where the road is if you really need it; a smattering of Zulu will prove invaluable.

Riverside to the old overnight stop

This section takes a little over an hour, and apart from the "four foot" drop immediately below Riverside Store, is the safest section on the river. It is here that the distance really starts getting to you and it is simply a matter of plodding on to the finish.

Old overnight stop to Mpompomani

Here you get a good warm-up for the second day. Some rapids are fairly large but not too difficult. A series of large waves and rapids heralds the approach to Mpompomani. This is best shot through a narrow slot on the extreme left of the rapid. You then move right to get to the inside of the right-hand corner at the bottom. There are some large waves here, but nothing to worry about if you have lined up correctly on the right-hand side.

Mpompomani to the waterfall

Mpompomani Rapid spits you out into long, calm pools interspersed with small, broad rapids. Twenty minutes later the river breaks up into several channels which should be treated with caution. One of them contains a new obstacle simply named "bad rapid", which formed during the 1987 floods.

The waterfall is recognisable on the right-hand side of the river as mist rises up from the boiling cauldron below. About 1 km above the fall, a road comes down to the river on the left bank. Stick to the left bank from here to the waterfall and portage over the rocks on the left.

Jane and Rory Pennefather show concern in Number One rapid in the Umkomaas marathon. (*The Natal Witness*)

Waterfall to Goodenough's Weir
Just 2 km after the falls lies Whirlpool, one of the meanest rapids on the river. It can be shot at most levels but is inclined to take the noses off doubles when low. It is best to portage on the left-hand bank unless you are particularly familiar with it.

The water spills over a ledge to the right, which you enter to the right of centre. On landing at the bottom, start moving left to negotiate the tight left corner half-way through the rapid. If all goes well it feels remarkably easy, but if things go wrong, it can mean a very nasty swim. The boiling frothy water makes it difficult to remain on the surface and a good, buoyant life-jacket is a necessity.

Half an hour later the river squeezes through Gulley Rapid; a tight right-hand corner in a narrow gulley-like channel. The sharp corner presents paddlers with problems and has been known to trap and break many a boat. A far safer way to negotiate this obstacle is to take the narrow gap immediately to the right of the main rapid.

Within a kilometre one is faced by No-name Rapid, a rocky, treacherous beast with no easy route through. It is perhaps safest to stick left and hope for the best.

Two kilometres later one approaches Goodenough's Weir, an obstacle which is possibly responsible for breaking more boats than all the other rapids on the river put together. This does not mean that it should be avoided at all costs; just be positive and keep control of your boat. The current is inclined to wash you where you don't want to go if you are unwary and moving too slowly.

The weir must be shot down the right shoot; anywhere else would be suicide. Approach at three-quarter pace just left of the centre of the shoot. Once you hit the stopper at the bottom, paddle as hard as you can in order to stay straight through the rocky rapid at the bottom of the weir.

The finish used to be at the bottom of this weir and one was pressurised by the announcer and expectant crowd into shooting. When the finish is positioned at the river mouth such pressure is no longer on one and a quick, easy portage exists on the left bank. Always remember that you are paddling your own canoe and that you make your own decisions. Shooting a rapid in order not to disappoint a crowd is all very generous of you, but breaking a boat worth a thousand rand is not much fun. It will add to the entertainment value of your act, but you will be left to replace your boat on your own.

Goodenough's Weir to the mouth

One or two inconspicuous rapids are all that remain between you and the finish. This flat, shallow, one-hour grind seems never-ending after the euphoria of the rapids. If the river is low, watch out for sand banks on the inside of corners. Just grin and bear it; it will soon be over and you can think back on the beauty and excitement of the past two days.

A K1 bucks in the waves of the Umkomaas. (Alick Rennie)

The Berg River marathon

This Western Province four-day marathon is one of the classic K1 races in the world. The standard is exceptionally high, for paddlers have to be fit to finish the 228 km course.

The Berg River meanders from Paarl through the Boland to the West Coast at Velddrif. One travels through the vineyards into the wheatlands and finally to the dry reaches of the West Coast. The change in scenery is sometimes enhanced by a backdrop of snow-clad mountains, adding a chill to an already cold river.

Besides being an exceptional canoe race, the Berg is revered for its incredible hospitality. Appropriately in this vineyard region, wine is freely available and often forms a fair portion of some paddlers' diets. All meals are also laid on by the organisers, thus removing many hassles for the canoeists and their seconds. Accommodation at the three overnight stops — Zonquas Drift, Bridgetown and Zoutkloof — is in farmers' barns, adding to the outstanding atmosphere.

The first two days take paddlers through palmiet bushes and over several weirs and rapids which demand a fair amount of river skill. The final two days are virtually flat, making wave riding one of the most important techniques needed.

Typical channels on day one of the Berg. (Alick Rennie)

Black rocks and brown water on the Buffalo in Natal. Every river has its own moods and sensations. (Alick Rennie)

The Commercial Road weir on the Duzi in Pietermaritzburg. The shute down the centre is rocky, hence the use of a white water boat to shoot it. (John Oliver)

The author takes a two metre fall on the Umzimkulu. By paddling fast over the lip, he manages to clear the stopper at the base of the falls.
(Val Adamson)

Shane Raw and Royston Swingewood successfully shoot a three metre fall in a K2, showing just how much a racing canoe can do in good hands.
(John Oliver)

A paddler skirts the stopper of Katryntjie's Drif. (Alick Rennie)

Weather conditions can vary tremendously, making an enormous difference to the difficulty of the race. Cold, wet days with a headwind can make the going exceptionally hard, calling for warm clothing and perseverance. One advantage to such conditions is that they are usually combined with a full river. This helps to shorten the time taken for the race. A low river is usually compensated for by warmer weather, and it simply becomes a case of hanging in there for several hours a day and tolerating the blisters and sore bum.

The Berg has seen several paddlers perform incredible feats, the most notable being those of Stefan Hugo, who has won the race five times. In his heyday he was perhaps the world's best long distance marathon racer and he is unlucky not to have won the Berg more often.

André Collins, another previous winner, has completed more than 20 Berg marathons, winning gold medals for finishing in the top 10 on almost every occasion. Sunley Uys, too, has performed exceptionally well through the years, helping to keep the victor's cup in the Western Province. A new generation of Province canoeists, including Mynhardt Marais, Donnie Malherbe and Robbie Clegg, are continuing this proud

Stefan Hugo, the most successful paddler ever in the Berg, in a position he is used to. (Alick Rennie)

tradition of the winelands. But their domination is under attack from paddlers to the north, with Greyling Viljoen, Graeme Montieth, Herman Chalupsky and Mark Perrow having taken the trophy away in recent years.

The times have seen many changes creep into the race with cash prizes, "hot spots" and new safety regulations being introduced. These hot spots or "speed primes" are certain marks on the route where the first paddler across earns about R1 000. Certain cut-off times are also included and any paddler who does not get to a point before the cut-off time is forced to retire. This, together with a limit on entries to 350 competent paddlers, has done much to increase the safety standards of the race. The insistence on canoe buoyancy and life-jackets when necessary has also improved the safety aspect.

For the serious long distance canoeist, this is a race not to be missed, for together with all its training it provides a background which will elevate you from mediocre to good.

The Breede

The second of the big western Cape events, this two-day marathon — like the Berg — displays typical Cape hospitality. It is predominantly a K2 race, and is often used as the venue for the South African K2 Championships. Being a fairly large, flat river with several weirs and few rapids, it is an ideal stretch for doubles racing.

An interesting change from the norm has been introduced to the race with the addition of a time trial section on the first day. Paddlers finish the first mass-start stage and then get set off one at a time for the last few kilometres of the first day. This gives the hard workers an advantage over the wave clingers as every crew races alone. A mass start is used again at the final stage on the second day.

The Breede Valley offers some of the finest scenery in the country, adding to the attraction of a most enjoyable race.

The Fish

The Fish River marathon has become one of the more popular races in South Africa. Cradock is the organisational cell of the race and is situated equidistant from the western Cape, Transvaal and Natal, making the race fairly easy to reach for all paddlers. Water is also guaranteed from Grassridge Dam, making the race attractive to paddlers from all over the country and it is consequently often used as the national marathon championship course.

The race starts on Grassridge Dam with paddlers going out and back from the wall before portaging into the river. The first day is strewn with obstacles, including low-level bridges, trees, weirs and rapids, but most of these are enjoyable rather than treacherous.

I first paddled this race in 1983, the second time it had ever been held, so it was a pretty new course to everyone there. Few paddlers had seen the river before the start, so it was a matter of running it blind in the race. The organisers had used a system of sign posting, with green signs where it was advisable to get out for an obstacle that could be shot and red signs to indicate portages around obstacles that could not. Such organisation made racing it an absolute pleasure, for all the decisions had already been taken for one. And some of the first day obstacles should certainly be avoided if they have not been scouted before.

Two obstacles on this race have become household names in canoeing families: Keith's Flyover and Cradock Weir. Only the brave can say these names without feeling a chill down the spine and sweaty palms on the paddles.

Keith's Flyover is reached on the first day, roughly 10 km after the start. It is a steep, narrow rapid through a slot in the rocks, with two to three stoppers that get bigger as you progress down it. The main problem is keeping upright in the aerated water. It is best avoided unless you have scouted it before the race. To survive it one needs a positive attitude. It appears best shot as far to the left as possible, although this is an opinion only, and some paddlers might have better ways of dealing with it.

Cradock Weir is the last obstacle in the race, cutting paddlers off from the finish when only minutes away from the line. I paddle the last day anxiously, knowing that Cradock Weir awaits me. The hard work of the past two days can be rewarded or nullified in one quick shoot. This weir has to be taken correctly or you will be punished accordingly.

It has long been the practice to shoot this weir at a slight angle to prevent the nose of the boat from sinking too deeply into the water below. As it is a sloping weir this is an orthodox method, but it has the danger of trapping one in the stopper below. For this reason I feel that one does better to shoot over almost straight but slowly to avoid the nose from going too deep. One is then able to paddle straight out of the pull-back without being held against the weir.

Cradock weir; one of the more awesome obstacles on the Fish. (John Oliver)

The Vaal

Not the race for slouches looking for a leisurely weekend's canoeing, the Vaal demands fitness and perseverance. The winners spend roughly nine hours on the water in the two days, so back-markers can be out there for a long time.

Starting from below the Vaal Dam wall, canoeists are confronted with 15 km of rapids before reaching the flat water which predominates in this race.

From the start, paddlers dash off towards the weirs and rapids, the most notable being the Shoot rapid and Visgat rapid and weir. The flats after this are deep and still to the overnight stop and then to the Barrage one hour into the second day.

From the Barrage portage to the finish in Parys, paddlers are confronted with a long and testing river section with numerous channels, shallow flats, weirs and rocky rapids. This is when it becomes vitally important to have drinking bottles, no holes, and thousands of miles of training behind you.

Its flattish nature and long distance make it a suitable K2 race although K1s do also compete.

The Vaal is one of the older marathons on the calendar, having been first raced back in the sixties. Together with the Berg and Duzi, it is one of the old classics in South African canoeing.

The Jukskei and Highveld Crocodile

The Jukskei and Highveld Crocodile are used for numerous races, the most prestigious being the Jukskei marathon. Like the Duzi, the Jukskei includes several long portages; in fact, it was designed with the Duzi in mind. Besides being a great race in itself, it gives paddlers a chance to prepare themselves for the Duzi, getting used to portaging, getting in and out and alternating paddling with running.

The Jukskei is a tributary of the Highveld Crocodile. The two rivers converge at a massive rapid several kilometres above Hartbeespoort Dam. The famous South African author Gordon Forster lived in a beautiful hideaway in the cliffs above the river and spent as much of his time helping out canoeists with wrapped boats as writing novels!

Being so close to Johannesburg and Pretoria the Jukskei and Crocodile rivers are well used by canoeists. This has led to problems of access as some farmers object to the hordes of paddlers travelling through their farms. Although a right of navigation exists to all South African rivers, do all you can to avoid confrontations and thus keep the river open to canoeists in the future.

The Lowveld Crocodile

The annual "Croc" marathon has waxed and waned in popularity over the years, the odd resident hippo near Nelspruit being responsible for the lowering of its popularity at times. The upper reaches mainly above the Montrose Falls are now used more and provide technical and picturesque canoeing.

The river is narrow and steep with continuous rapids. Low-level bridges abound so capsizing and rolling under them has become a time-saving practice for experienced paddlers.

Both days of the two-day marathon are relatively short (33 km and 36 km respectively) as far as South African marathons go, so it is a race that appeals to the shorter distance rough water paddlers. Hence names such as Jerome Truran and Sean Rice appear on the winner's trophy.

Its fast-flowing nature also makes it a suitable river for white water and slalom racing. Before the growth in popularity of the Bushman's in Natal, it was often the venue for the SA white water and slalom championships.

Shorter long distance events

Besides these better known marathons, numerous shorter events are held, differing in length from three and four-hour grinds to races of less than an hour.

In the summer rainfall region — Natal, Transvaal and the OFS — long distance racing starts in August or September, culminating in January or February when the rivers are at their fullest.

In the western Cape, races start in May in preparation for the Berg marathon in July. The season continues until the Breede marathon in September.

The shorter events have become very popular as they do not demand the time and effort of the multi-day marathons. Many of the provincial and national championship races are single-day events, for it is felt that pure canoeing skill can be measured as well in a short race as in a long one. River knowledge is less important in most of the shorter races, so they are a fairer reflection on visiting paddlers who are less familiar with the river.

Relay races

Relay races are popular as part of L.D. races. Two main types of relays occur. In the river relays, teams of four compete. They use a K1, a K2 and a wild water racer. Usually the first rough section of about 5 km is covered in a white water boat, followed by 10 km for the K1 and a final 10 km or further for the K2. On the flatter rivers such as the Western Province Berg, white water boats are replaced by K1s.

The second type of relay is held on flat water. These "enduro" events are raced on time: they are 8, 10 or 12 hours long, with the team covering the greatest distance being the winner. Teams usually consist of four paddlers who are free to use K1s, K2s or K4s. Obviously K4s are quickest but give paddlers no rest, and no one can keep going non-stop at a good pace for 10 hours. Teams therefore have to decide which boats will give them the best balance between speed and exhaustion.

Some relays are restricted to the use of K1s or K2s only, which is a better reflection on the ability of teams.

Long distance canoeing in South Africa is primarily a river canoeing sport. Flat water races are the exception rather than the rule. In Europe the converse is true. Many blame river canoeing for the supposed poor international marathon racing standard of our paddlers, for they are learning the skills of white water rather than training for flats.

World championships are now held in canoe marathon racing. The marathon route consists of a flat 42 km course with two portages. With the possibility of our acceptance back into the international canoeing world, our marathon racing needs to conform to the international model.

But long distance canoe racing in South Africa attracts more paddlers than canoe racing anywhere else in the world and this is largely because of its exciting river racing nature. Our races suit our type of rivers; flat water racing and portaging are suited to canals and locks.

"International marathon" racing is being introduced here, but in addition to the present racing system. Having both river L.D. and flat 42 km marathon races provides the paddlers with an extremely large selection of long distance-type races.

9 WHERE TO GO CANOEING

Such is the versatility of canoes that they can be used almost anywhere. Water is advisable but not absolutely necessary. Canoes have been utilised as bobsleighs and toboggans and their durability is so great that water simply assists as a lubricant. Paddlers have been known to slide several hundred metres down rocky slopes in order to get to a river, for rough water canoeists are notoriously lazy about using their legs.

It is best to start canoeing on a stretch of water that is calm and sheltered, especially if you have an unstable racing craft. Wind affects not only stability but also steering. Shorter canoes can be used in swimming pools for the clear water provides the perfect conditions for practising certain strokes and the Eskimo roll.

The value of a swimming pool for canoeing is often overlooked. Besides being the ideal place to learn technique, it can provide a certain amount of pleasure. The water is clean, so visibility is good. A capsized paddler can watch the paddle to see what he is doing when practising the Eskimo roll. A novice can learn to roll within half an hour in a pool under supervision, whereas learning in the river can take months.

The polo-bat is the ideal kayak to use in a pool. It is short, slow and manoeuvrable, making it suited to the limited space. Canoe polo is played in these boats with teams of four on a side flicking and throwing the ball about. The boats are covered along the outer gunwhale line with a thick strip of rubber to protect the pool from bashes.

Slalom canoes and paddle-skis are also suitable in pools for they are short and turn well. I find the paddle-ski the ideal craft on which to teach the Eskimo roll for it does not fill up with water or need a spray cover. It must have a seat belt to keep the paddler in position whilst rolling, but if the paddler fails, he can release the belt and fall off. He then simply climbs back on and tightens the belt again. It is, however, unnecessary for the paddler to fall off the ski even when he cannot roll upright for an assistant in the water can always help him back up.

Several activities in the pool help to improve the paddler's skills, especially for slalom and rough water canoeists. Buoys positioned in the pool create a squiggly obstacle course. By using efficient strokes, paddlers are able to improve their times in negotiating the course.

Slalom poles can be strung above the pool, creating a mini slalom course. An exercise that was once popular with slalomists was a "wiggle test". This involved negotiating the same gate several times from different sides and from different directions. The fact that this was a standard exercise made it possible for canoeists to compare their performances with those of other canoeists. Its value to slalom training is now considered dubious, but for those who wish to compare their gate technique with the best slalomists in the world, most British canoeing books describe them. If you can complete the course in less than a minute, you should consider specialising in slalom. If more than one gate can be strung above the pool, it is of greater value to work out a course with several different approaches to the gate than to do the wiggle test.

The pool is also an ideal place for practising certain strokes, capsizing, getting into your boat in deep water and rescue techniques. Again, rather than describe the laborious methods of emptying and re-entering a canoe in deep water, I recommend that paddlers read books such as *Living Canoeing* by Alan Byde or *Canoeing Complete* edited by Brian Skilling.

For paddlers wishing to get a feel for waterfalls, the canoe can be launched from a high diving board. This also prepares one for seal launches off high banks into the river.

Yet despite all these ways of adding interest to pool canoeing, true paddling takes place on wild and open waters. Apart from canoe polo, which is a sport in its own right, pool canoeing should never be seen as

Canoe polo – rugby on water and you are armed with a paddle. (Val Adamson)

more than a means to an end. Novices can receive excellent coaching in a pool; paddlers can brush up and do a certain amount of training; but the ultimate aim of time spent in a pool is to improve one's canoeing when one is out on the river.

But moving onto the river too soon can be a costly, boat-breaking and heart-breaking experience. Often the larger, wind-swept dams are more difficult than the calmer river sections for the waves strike the boat from all angles. Thus canoeing in windy conditions on a dam has great value for it puts your balance to the test without risking your boat to the rocks in the event of a capsize.

River waves are taken straight on from the front. This makes balancing in rapids fairly easy as long as you keep up your speed. Not all parts of the country provide the paddler with perfect beginner conditions, but a cautious approach and sufficient self-discipline to force yourself to portage tricky sections should make it possible for you to paddle some good water without risking damage to yourself and your canoe.

It is sometimes said that South Africa as a country lacks beautiful, large, clean rivers for canoeing. Travellers expound the beauties of European and New Zealand rivers, the Zambezi, the Colorado and many others without ever having seen the beautiful streams that spill out of the Cape fold mountains or the unknown hidden rivers in the valleys of Natal. They base their sweeping statements on their experiences of the Duzi, without having touched the several thousand kilometres of canoeing waterways in the rest of the country. Certainly other areas in southern Africa and abroad offer a beauty that South Africa might not have, but a remarkable number of beautiful and unknown rivers lie as yet unexplored, waiting for intrepid explorers to savour their delights.

The river sections described below are mentioned in order of difficulty to give the canoeist an idea of where to go according to his degree of canoeing expertise. Many of the sections are used for long distance racing as they provide good canoeing without excessive danger or risk of damage to boats.

The sections mentioned are only some of the better known ones and there are many unknown and unused rivers for the canoeist to explore. Part of the pleasure of canoeing is its exploratory nature. Any canoeist who is inquisitive enough can find an as yet unpaddled section of river in this country and be the first to conquer it.

Tips about river conditions should be treated with circumspection, for non-canoeing locals are inclined to confuse local myths with facts and give very misleading advice. Rather try the local canoeists, if there are any. They can be a store of useful information, but do not take what they say as gospel for experienced canoeists have a habit of seeing everything as easy just because it is so to them. You are your best guide to the suitability of a river for your canoeing. Learn to look at a rapid from the bank, and decide for yourself whether it is possible to shoot it.

It is simply not possible in one small chapter to do justice to all the suitable canoeing waters in the four provinces of South Africa. Many books could be written on rivers alone so only some are included here.

Natal

As the wettest and steepest province in the country, Natal has a large number of canoeable rivers. A good holiday for non-Natal canoeists would be to spend a couple of weeks in the summer staying in and near Pietermaritzburg, travelling out to the rivers each day. Paddlers can experience a variety of sections all within easy reach, and the country hotels provide accommodation close to the rivers where a casual holiday atmosphere exists. There is nothing to make the rapids feel bigger and your episodes of the day feel braver than a few pints in a pub in the evening.

Easy sections for the beginner

The best sections for the beginner to try in a river are the open, rockless stretches. They must not be too shallow, for a capsize should allow the boat to float along unhindered. Trees in particular should be avoided.

1. Upper Umgeni: Albert Falls Dam to Gum Trees (16 km)

The section of this river near the Greytown Road Bridge is referred to as the upper Umgeni to differentiate it from the Umgeni of the Duzi marathon course or lower Umgeni. There are, however, canoeable sections further upstream.

From directly below Albert Falls Dam, one paddles approximately 16 km to Gum Trees. The rapids are of grade 1 or 2 and present few problems. Allow one to two hours to complete this pleasant and easy paddle.

The first obstacle at the put-in, the Albert Falls Weir, is the largest and most difficult obstacle on the course. Shoot it on the extreme left approximately half a metre from the bank as rocks below obstruct the more obvious-looking routes just slightly further right.

The 4 km to the Greytown Road Bridge consist of small, easy rapids and a few channels through mulberry trees. They present very few problems as the current is slow.

Another 5 km of flat water takes you to the start of the main section of rapids. This series of grade 2 drops is relatively simple. You can check your decision making by trying to choose the correct channels through the islands. The best ones are fairly obvious and there is not much wrong with the wrong ones.

These rapids are interspersed with a few shallow pools which eventually take you to the Gum Trees flats. This long, deep pool is also ideal for flat water paddling and is used by many Pietermaritzburg canoeists for training.

Lower Umgeni

2. Umfula Store to Inanda Dam (15 km)
Best paddled when the river is full, this section presents a maze of sandbanks in low water. The rapids are grade 2 and fairly easy to read. This stretch gives one good practice at reading sandbanks and finding the deep water. It forms the latter part of the second day of the Duzi marathon.

3. Pumphouse Weirs to Durban (12 km)
The river is predominantly flat, but a few small rapids near the beginning provide some excitement. Included here is Dog's Leg, a sharp and rocky right-hand turn in a rapid. It has become easier in recent years and should not present any difficulty. The final few kilometres into Durban are on the tidal stretch of the Blue Lagoon.

4. The Duzi
This polluted little river still has much to recommend it. Firstly, it is easily accessible as it flows through Pietermaritzburg. It also has the large Camp's Drift Canal in the town, one of the most used pieces of water in the country, and the rapids on the section down to Duzi Bridge, the first night's stop on the Duzi marathon, are challenging without being difficult.

For Pietermaritzburg canoeists the section from the Camp's Drift Canal down to the low-level bridge near the SPCA offers an ideal introduction to river canoeing. Shoot down the steps of the Ernie Pearce Weir, but the Commercial Road Weir is best avoided until you have gained experience. The broken down Musson's Weir is also best portaged as it contains several sharp rocks in awkward places.

Once you feel more confident, progress to the lower section of the Duzi from Campbell's Farm to Duzi Bridge. This will involve several long portages, so unless you are planning on racing the Duzi canoe marathon, you will no doubt find other sections of river to learn on.

5. The Umzimkulu-Underberg: Hatcheries to Scotston Bridge (13 km)
From Underberg village, the Drakensberg towers tantalisingly near, beckoning one to explore its parks and valleys. Myriad streams flow off the slopes, filling the Umzimkulu with canoeing's purest water.

The river becomes suitably canoeable at the trout hatcheries on the Drakensberg Gardens road. From here it meanders across a fairly flat plain, providing small rapids and a few easy channels around islands. A weir half a metre high at Taylor's Farm can be shot on the left, but it should be studied from the bank first as some shallow rocks immediately below it can damage the nose of a boat.

The beginner can paddle on from here to Scotston Bridge immediately below Underberg. A few larger rapids occur on the section to the bridge from the weir, but are not too dificult for the novice. The whole section is 13 km long, which is ideal for a morning or afternoon paddle. The gorge below Scotston Bridge also provides excellent canoeing but is more difficult than the upper reaches and is best paddled once one has gained some experience. (It is described later.)

Sections for those with a bit of experience

The Umgeni: Gum Trees to Edmonds' Farm (20 km)

Apart from providing excellent canoeing, this stretch of the river flows through one of the most secluded and unspoilt gorges in the country. It is bound by towering sandstone cliffs which form a natural barrier to despoilation. Numerous species of birds inhabit the natural forest which clings to the steep-sided slopes. The paddler would do well to slow off in a tranquil pool and enjoy this unspoilt valley.

The river provides continuous grade 2 and 3 rapids. They are fairly shallow and rocky for most of the year and so present little danger, but a canoe can easily be damaged. Try to paddle here when the river is flowing well and go with someone who knows the way. Use a strong canoe that can take a fair amount of bashing about.

Take the deepest channel whenever the river splits, but there are certain parts which need to be learnt. If you are planning to race successfully down this section, then it is necessary to learn the way beforehand.

The Umkomaas: Number 8 Rapid to St Josephine's Bridge (12 km)

Described under the Umkomaas marathon section, this part of the river provides the big water experience without any dangers. The river is deep and open with large waves. Many are as easily swum through as paddled and a capsized canoe (packed with buoyancy) floats along unhindered by rocks. Nevertheless, there are some rapids which should be treated with respect especially when the river is full.

The Umzimkulu-Underberg Gorge (12 km)

The section of this river described earlier is tranquil, but soon after Scotston Bridge a testing weir spans the route. This weir is best portaged on the right but can be safely shot down the right shoot when very full. All weirs are potentially hazardous, and few more so than this one. If the right shoot is not working, the braver paddlers can shoot down as far left as possible, about 1,5 m from the bank. This is really only necessary in a race if you are serious about doing well, otherwise the easy portage is best.

Two kilometres after the weir, the river enters the gorge. Medium-sized rapids (grade 2 to 3) abound and all are shootable. There are few channels so route-finding is easy. The obvious way is always the best. Some of these rapids provide the relative beginner with one of the safest yet more exciting sections of rough water to be found. The gorge is the ideal introduction to rough water canoeing.

After the gorge 2 km of flats carry one to the Coleford Road Bridge. This is the finish of the annual Underberg race and a suitable spot for the tripper to end his excursion.

Being so near its source, the Umzimkulu lacks volume in this upper section during a dry spell, so it is best paddled after heavy rains.

The Umzimkulu: Centecow Mission to Stokes's Farm (18 km)

A long distance race is held from Centecow Mission to Stokes' Farm, a distance of 18 km. The first two and last five kilometres have grade 2 to 3 rapids while the middle section is relatively flat with grade 1 and 2 rapids. Two kilometres from the end is a massive grade 4/5 fall, which a surprising number of paddlers shoot in the race. A surprising number also break their boats! It is a good section to learn on for the rapids are not large, but they demand a fair amount of reading from the top and manoeuvring within.

There are also several other good canoeing sections nearby, both on the Umzimkulu and Ngwagwane. Paddlers planning to spend some time in the area should go prepared with racing and tripping craft, for a remarkable variety of river conditions is found.

Mooi River town to Sierra Ranch (20 km)

This rather flat section of river has a sprinkling of challenging rapids especially in the final 4 km before the ranch. A low-level bridge on a dirt road which turns off the main Mooi River—Greytown road gives access to the river at the 15 km mark.

If you are more interested in paddling on flat water, get out at this bridge, but if your interest is in rapids, paddle from here to Sierra Ranch. The first kilometre after the bridge is fairly flat, but the final four kilometres are continuous grade 2 rapids. Be careful not to be carried over the small waterfall at the finish. It is hard to recognise from the top so go cautiously. You do not finish at the ranch itself but rather 5 km away in the middle of nowhere. Ask at the ranch for the road to the river.

Sections for the more experienced

Umgeni: Confluence section (5 km)

Some of the largest and most exciting rapids used in long distance racing are found from the Duzi confluence to Ibis Point Rapid on the Umgeni. This is a section that is used only by Duzi paddlers, for it is inaccessible by road, although a short walk upstream from Ibis Point to the Washing Machine Rapid is a good way for the rough water enthusiast to get to it.

The first rapid, the Washing Machine, is aptly named as those who have been caught in the stopper on the right can tell you. A more sensible shoot is down the "steps" in the middle left, or if it is full enough, slide down the rock in the centre.

The next kilometre consists of grade 2/3 rapids that are easily shot. The last monster of the section is the double rapid of Slide and Ibis Point. Both are best shot down the right and are easier than they appear. If portaged (as they should be in the Duzi marathon, unless you are experienced) there is a quick route through the bush on the right.

Willem's Shoot down the right of both rapids is the fastest route down, but it requires some canoeing gymnastics as you slide dry over various rock shelves.

The Ibis Point Weir, a few hundred metres after the rapid, is best avoided, especially in a K2. It has a habit of breaking boats at the front cockpit. A single is less affected, but perhaps the best way to shoot it is sideways to avoid knocking the nose of the boat down so hard. This method requires a great deal of experience, and I would prefer to see someone else do it before I give it a try!

Umkomaas: Hella-hella to the sea (140 km)

All sections on the Umkomaas from Hella-hella to the sea are described in detail in Chapter 8 as they form the Umkomaas marathon route. For long distance racing the Umkomaas ranks in my books as the most enjoyable stretch of water used.

Few experiences match the mixture of anxiety and exhilaration one feels on arriving at Hella-hella Bridge to see a full, brown river pulsating below. Any reading on the measuring line above four means that you are in for one of the most exciting rides canoeing has to offer.

Make sure that your boat is packed with buoyancy and that you are wearing a good, buoyant life-jacket. Paddle off in confident mood, as like a horse, the river will sense if you are nervous!

Hug the right bank of the main stream down the first series of rapids. They are big but manageable and warm you up for Number 1 rapid, which lies 2 km after the bridge.

It starts with a rock ledge that should be taken towards the left when the river is full. You then enter a series of waves that get bigger and bigger as the rapid progesses until it spills you into a large, long pool. Once you have survived this testing introduction your confidence will grow tremendously and you will be ready to take on the many large rapids that lie between you and the sea.

Bushman's River

The Bushman's is one of the most used rivers in Natal. It provides continuous rapids on most sections and has become the home of white water and slalom racing in South Africa. It is easily accessible and usually has water guaranteed from Wagondrift Dam for competitions.

Although some sections above the dam are canoeable, the most enjoyable stretches are to be found below the town of Estcourt. The first 5 km below Lambert Park form the white water course and together with the next 15 km to the Weenen Road, the Bushman's long distance race.

The entire 20 km present tricky grade 3 rapids with a few fast-flowing pools. Most rapids can be "read" from the top and are best shot in the most obvious places. The section is suitable for racing K1s and K2s, but rough water skills can be learnt and more enjoyment had in slalom and white water boats, especially over the white water course.

Black Rock and Heaven and Hell rapids are the two used as slalom sites. Both are fast flowing with few rocks or obstacles, making them ideal for slalom racing training.

Umzimkulu: Pholela to Centecow (10 km)

This steep and rocky section offers some fine white water when full. Some of the rapids drop several metres in as little distance, forming large and powerful waves and whipping you along at tremendous speed.

When low, this stretch is a bit of a rock bash but still has some interesting slots in the rocks for those who wish to try them. A strong white water, slalom or plastic boat is best suited to this section.

Any novice paddler wanting to get a fair amount of rough water experience would do well to start here, for the rapids are big but not frighteningly so. One or two of the larger ones are easily portaged.

Umzimkulu: Stokes's Farm to Islington Store (30 km)

From the finish of the Creighton canoe race to Islington, one finds a magnificent stretch of river with grade 3 to 4 rapids and several waterfalls. Essentially suitable for plastic boats, it is also enjoyable in slalom and white water kayaks.

As one takes to the water at Stokes's Farm, the ominous rumble of a 2 m fall wafts upstream. A fine spray can be seen rising from the fall, beckoning the way for the brave. The fall is absolutely straight and easy to shoot on the left-hand side. The plunge pool below is deep and still and the stopper is easily cleared with a bit of speed. Only the natural fear of dropping over a ledge as high as a canoe is long presents an obstacle. Once a paddler has shot such a fall, further shoots become routine. A side shoot on the extreme right where the fall is broken into a couple of ledges presents a more orthodox but less easy route.

Two kilometres further, a 45 degree sloping waterfall about 3 m high is easily shot on the right. The paddler is completely immersed in the rather large stopper below, but pops up easily enough out of its grip. I once tried to take a photograph of a canoe shooting this drop to illustrate how it disappeared, but unfortunately the canoe was underwater when I clicked the shutter and nothing but the fall appears in the print!

The third fall is 4 m high and absolutely straight on the left-hand side. On the right is a sloping shoot with a 60 degree gradient. Until recently, such a fall was considered "un-canoeable" by all paddlers, but since the emergence of Marco Begni, Jerome Truran, Tim Biggs, Phillip Lloyd, Bruce Yelland and a few others as white water experts, such falls are being viewed with braver eyes. Having gained their experience on the world's greatest rivers, including the Amazon, Colorado, Zambezi and Zaire, they can cope with the larger local obstacles.

The following fall is a definite no-no. It is many metres high and includes a gorge and rapid that are frightening but spectacular to view. Known as Cooper's Falls, they house a defunct hydro-electric plant and are a popular attraction in the Creighton area.

Pull up in the right-hand channel at the top of the fall and walk over the island to view the gorge. The river enters the 4 m wide chasm through a suicidal grade 6 rapid and the water then boils through the "pool", bound on either side by straight rock sides. Finally it spills over a 15 m drop into the plunge pool below.

Dave Walker, a paddler with two decades of river tripping experience in southern Africa, once described this fall as the most impressive he had ever seen. Even for the paddler who is unable to paddle this section, a drive to the fall is well worthwhile.

The portage down the right bank to the river below is fairly hard, although the canoe can be left to slide down the grassy slopes on its own.

From here excellent canoeing is to be found with continuous large rapids for several kilometres. Part of this section was used for the South African White Water Championships in the 1970s, but it led to controversy for some of the rapids were considered too big! The rapid that was mainly to blame has since been made easy by the 1987 floods, so the stretch has improved somewhat.

It contains a series of steep and twisting ledges, fast shoots with massive waves and several steep rapids where the paddler has to weave from side to side in order to miss the stoppers. It is best paddled full when one has to think very quickly and manoeuvre around continuously, but none of the rapids presents any danger so the section can be thoroughly enjoyed by the improving wild water paddler.

Sections for the experienced white water tripper

The experienced white water tripper invariably uses a plastic canoe as its durability is vitally important in dealing with harsh and rocky conditions. He finds suitable rivers by looking for large volumes and steep gradients. Some of the sections that appeal to him are described below.

Umgeni Valley Game Ranch (20 km)

The gorge below Howick Falls is one of the steepest and most taxing to be found in Natal. The Umgeni is rather small here, depending of course on how much water is released from Midmar Dam. The gradient and small volume create mountain stream conditions where the paddler has to react extremely quickly to cope with the continuous steep drops and rapids.

One can gain access either by climbing down the path at Howick Falls or driving into the game ranch and embarking a couple of kilometres further downstream. The latter route helps one avoid a couple of small waterfalls which have been shot but are neither safe nor easy.

The first few kilometres of this section are the roughest, for as the river nears Albert Falls Dam, it levels out. The pick-up point at Morton's Drift is easily accessible, being on a good road only 20 km from Pietermaritzburg.

Umkomaas: Deepdale to Hella-hella (35 km)
One of the classic rough water trips, this section provides eight hours of unrelenting grade 4 rapids with the odd grade 5 thrown in for good measure. It can be paddled at low and high levels, for the gradient provides excitement even when volume is lacking. When full, it should be tackled only by experienced canoeists, for it is a fast and dangerous river for the unwary. Shooting the notorious 15 m high Deepdale Falls, first achieved by Marco Begni in 1988, must rank with going over Niagara in a barrel. Begni split his "indestructible" plastic canoe open on these falls, yet despite this, they have been shot successfully several times since.

The grade 4 rapids start below the waterfall and take you through to Hella-hella. Several rapids, like the notorious Long Drop, fall more than 10 m from top to bottom over a distance of 50 m. Much scouting from the bank is necessary and paddlers should not feel pressured into shooting a rapid which they feel is too difficult for them.

Umzimkulu: Thrombosis Gorge (25 km)
This rather daunting name came into existence through the experiences of trout fishermen who found the steep climb in and out of the gorge heavy going. But it is also an appropriate name for the canoeist as the gorge offers some frighteningly steep, tight and rocky rapids. Like the Deepdale—Hella-hella section, it is best tackled for the first time when relatively low.

A 10 m fall on this section has also been shot by Begni, but the slow and difficult alternative route down the left bank is better suited to most paddlers. If you have a rescue throw-rope, your canoe can be let down the side and you can jump into the plunge pool below. This is rather fun and presents no risks.

One can be picked up at the confluence of the Umzimkulu and Pholela rivers, easily accessible either from Centecow Mission or Bulwer.

The Tugela
As the second largest river in South Africa and with a steeper gradient than many large rivers, the Tugela offers some of the most exciting rough water canoeing in the country. Conditions along its 500 km length obviously vary but in general it is a fast-flowing river with big waves and open rapids.

Perhaps the most popular parts to canoeists are the sections from below Colenso to Weenen and Tugela Ferry to Jamieson's Drift. Several river running companies take touring groups down the latter section in rubber dinghies and tupperware kayaks. It is ideal for this as the secluded valley, white sandbanks and plentiful driftwood provide perfect camping conditions which add to the lure of excellent canoeing.

When the river is full, some of the biggest river waves in the country are to be found here. Waves formed as though designed for looping, surfing and popping out abound. One can spend hours in a single rapid just playing about, so it is best to paddle this section with time to spare. Try and set a soft target with only a few kilometres a day to be covered so that most of a day can be spent leisurely in one place.

The warmth and beauty of this valley have a strangely narcotic effect on the paddler and can lull him into a false sense of security. This has its dangers, for some of the rapids on this section can be treacherous if underestimated.

On the Tugela marathon route on the lower sections of the river from Middeldrift to Mandini the river is much more open with less gradient but a larger volume, providing open rapids with massive waves. A canoe can travel along at a whacking pace and as long as the spray covers are good, little is likely to go wrong. A swim can be unpleasant, however, as the river is broad and reaching the bank can take a long time in the swiftly flowing water.

The many large tributaries of the Tugela together with its source waters provide as yet untapped possibilities for canoeing pleasure. During a wet summer, the Drakensberg streams such as the Bushman's, Umlambonja, Mhlwazini and the Tugela itself carry large volumes of water down the lower slopes of the mountain, providing exciting white water possibilities.

Transvaal

The Highveld Crocodile

Mark Perrow

Most canoeing in the Transvaal is done on the Jukskei and Highveld Crocodile rivers, not only because of their suitability, but also their proximity to Johannesburg and Pretoria. The Jukskei is a tributary of the Crocodile, and the latter is not paddled above the confluence, so the two rivers are usually considered as one. The following descriptions of various sections are supplied by Mark Perrow, a paddler with a sound knowledge of canoeing rivers in the Transvaal.

Winsome to Broederstroom (13 km)

This relatively easy section for the beginner is characterised by flat pools regularly interspersed with small, rocky rapids.

Two kilometres below Winsome Valley you come across the first real obstacle, Constantia Rapid. It can be shot on the left when the river is low, and on the right when full, but a quick and easy portage can be made down the right bank. Hennops Weir, 1 km further downstream, is a definite portage, done on the right.

Just beyond half-way down this section, you come across Rambo's Bridge. When the river is very low, you can squeeze through the pipes below the bridge, just right of centre, but when it is running fuller, take out on the left and put back in on the right. Try to make as little noise as possible as landowners on the left have been known to shoot at paddlers on their land. When the river is full, paddle straight over the top of the bridge.

Approximately 10 km from the start is the first of the Pelindaba weirs. It is recommended that you portage this over a metre-high portage on the right. The safest place to shoot the weir is on the right. Take it at an angle of 45 degrees facing right to left.

At the second Pelindaba weir 200 m further downstream, an easy shoot can be made in the middle down the stairs. Alternatively it can be portaged on the left.

Canoeists must take out at the pleasure resort below the Broederstroom Road Bridge as they are not welcome at the campsite on the left!

Friday's Farm to Winsome Valley (6 km)

This is probably the trickiest section of the Crocodile. Some really interesting rapids are found here when the river is full, but it is a bit of a boat cruncher when the river is low. The section is characterised by tight, tricky rapids, none more so than the confluence rapid. Here the Jukskei and Crocodile rivers merge, approximately 3 km from the start. It is best to take out at the big rock on the left and follow the path 500 m downstream. The rapid can be shot either down the right or in the centre.

Lanseria to Friday's Farm (9 km)

About 500 m of flat water carries one to the Lanseria Waterfall. The rocky drop can be shot just left of middle, or down the easy chicken run on the right when the river is up.

One comes upon the first weir soon afterwards. It can be quickly portaged on the left or shot down the chicken run on the right when the river is up. Shoot the smaller second weir on the extreme left!

Friday's Weir lies 1 km above the take-out point. It is best to portage on the right, although it can be shot if one is prepared to put one's boat at risk. Approach it on the extreme right at 45 degrees and face from right to left.

The Vaal
Mark Perrow
Traditionally the most used and best known inland waterway in the country, the Vaal provides hundreds of kilometres of canoeable water. Most of it is flat, but certain sections can offer Colorado-type paddling when in flood. Transvaal canoeist Peter Wise told me of a rubber dinghy race down the rapids of Parys when the river was in flood, and he swears that the water was rougher and more dangerous than the Zambezi Gorge!

Such conditions are uncharacteristic of the Vaal as most canoeists know it, however, and the section from Vaal Dam to Parys, used for the classic Vaal marathon, is the part frequently used by paddlers. Mark Perrow describes it and offers advice.

Vaal Dam to Groenoewers
The success of this trip depends on the amount of water being released from the dam. Vaal rocks are much sharper than those on the Crocodile and can cut straight through a fibreglass canoe.

After 100 m of flat water one comes to Kloppers' Rapid, which creates an exciting and chaotic start to the various races which begin here. After another 2 km one reaches the first weir, which is easily portaged on the left or right bank. It can be shot, but as a renowned boat breaker, it is best avoided by all but the more experienced. If you shoot, approach 1 m from the left pillar of the right channel, or alternatively drop over sideways in the middle of the weir.

The Shute is approximately 7 km from the dam and is one of the more enjoyable rapids on the river. The entire Vaal narrows into a 5 m wide gap, resulting in large standing waves. It is best shot through the middle over the waves, for in that way one avoids the swirling eddies on either side of the main current.

Vischgat is the trickiest rapid on the Vaal marathon route. It can be shot down the main drop on the right or the chicken runs in the middle or extreme left. The portage is unfortunately slow because of the uneven terrain.

The 6 km from Vischgat to Groenoewers are relatively flat with a few shallow rapids.

The upper stretches of the Vaal are characterised by many channels and islands, which makes choosing the best route difficult. The general rule is to follow the largest flow of water.

Groenoewers to Barrage (60 km)
The next 60 km are absolutely flat apart from a small weir half a metre high at the pumphouse, 10 km downstream from Groenoewers.

Markerboards every kilometre on the left bank from the pumphouse to the Barrage give paddlers an idea of the distance they have travelled. This deep waterway with its numerous access and vantage points on banks and bridges make it a well-used race section, suitable to both paddlers and spectators.

Barrage to Parys (44 km)

This relatively easy stretch is characterised by many channels. These have to be learnt by anyone who hopes to do well on this section. Long, flat pools are interspersed with shallow rapids, the trickiest being the 800 m long Benoude Boude. It is situated about 12 km downstream from the Barrage. Just follow the main flow of water and wind your way through the channels.

A few kilometres below this rapid is a metre-high weir which can be shot on the left or portaged over the rocks in the middle. From here to Parys it is plain sailing, the main task being the choosing of the correct channels. When in doubt apply the golden rule: follow the bulk of the water.

The only access point to this stretch of river is at Van Heerden's Farm, 18 km below the Barrage. It is a good spot to know of should things go wrong, although paddlers are unlikely to have problems on this section.

Cape Province

The western Cape

Tim Biggs

The Berg and Breede rivers in the south-western Cape are used extensively for long distance canoe racing and provide ideal canoeing waters for paddlers in K1 and K2 craft. No sections are dangerous, but the beginner on the Berg should be careful of trees on the first day of the race.

The following section is written by Tim Biggs, a Springbok canoeist and previous Duzi winner with a vast amount of white water experience. He was one of the first paddlers to explore the source waters of the Amazon in Peru and also has a thorough knowledge of rivers in the western Cape.

The mountainous Alpine-type streams of the south-western Cape offer adventurous plastic boaters many world class runs and adrenalin kicks. In sharp contrast to the lazy long distance rivers such as the Berg and Breede, these rivers have very steep gradients, they often require highly technical paddling, and have breathtakingly spectacular scenery and rock formations.

There are, however, some drawbacks to these rivers:
- They are generally low in volume (± 10–15 cumecs) and only fuller than this immediately after rain.

- The south-western Cape is a winter rainfall area, so rivers can only be paddled in the colder months. Good paddling gear and wet suits are generally necessary.
- Many of the rivers require permits for access, which can be difficult to acquire.

Probably the most significant factor concerning these Cape rivers is their extreme and erratic fluctuations in water flow. Conditions can vary from low volume "pool-drop"-type descents to the most viciously turbulent descents imaginable.

The Palmiet River

The organically brown-stained waters of the Palmiet take kayakers through some of the country's most beautiful fynbos and Table Mountain sandstone scenery. This 25 km stretch with an approximate gradient of 10 m/km is ideal for the intermediate standard paddler.

Access is from Elgin and the put-in is found below the dams. The trip begins with palmiet-choked sections of river with grade 2 and 3 rapids, but gradually opens out into pleasant grade 3 and 4 water. Approximately two-thirds of the way down is a spectacular cataract (with an approximately 10 m vertical drop) which has, as yet, not been run. The take-out to this enjoyable one-day trip is at the mouth at Kleinmond, on the Indian Ocean.

The Molenaars River

Only one hour's drive from Cape Town along the N1, kayakers can confidently fit in an afternoon's paddling down this stretch of grade 3 and 4 rapids. This trip starts immediately below the Du Toit's Kloof tunnel and ends some 12 km downstream alongside the N1. There is also the option of a pit-stop at the riverside Du Toit's Kloof Motel.

The average gradient is approximately 15 m/km and this stretch can be enjoyed by the average rough water paddler as well as the "hotties", especially by the latter when full.

Visgat Kloof on the Olifants River

This is certainly the country's most impressive "kloofing"-type river for kayaking. The unique stretch of river offers both intermediate and skilled paddlers a weekend's tripping second to none.

Although the 18 km section can be run as a single-day trip, its distance from towns and its difficult access makes a two-day trip more favourable. The 35 m/km gradient and highly technical grade 3 to 5 rapids make scouting and good safety back-up essential.

As with many of the Cape rivers, it was rock climbers such as Butch de Bruin, Tony Dick and Rich Smithers who introduced kayakers to this amazing gorge, which in places is narrower than a paddle width!

The river already sports numerous wild tales of epic trips: bad swims, big eyes, bigger parties and midnight floods, all of which contribute to a truly classic trip.

The Dwars River
The Dwars River, main tributary to the Breede, is deceptively calm and innocent as it swirls through the Cederberg town of Ceres.
If you aren't afraid of heights it is a fine stretch to run, with the first 10 km comprising grade 4 and 5 rapids, drops and waterfalls. The climax to this section is a spectacular 10 m waterfall, first run by myself (see colour photos).
The average gradient over this stretch is approximately 35 m/km but the initial 5 km are much steeper than this.

The Wit
At first sight from Baines Pass the Wit looks like an interesting run — but actually get down to river level and it is outrageous! It falls approximately 45 m/km over 10 km, and is without doubt one of the country's premier runs. It is suitable for skilled paddlers only and sports continuous grade 4 and 5 rapids, siphons and undercuts, and is absolutely wild when full.

Cape alpine rivers for future generations
Current wild water paddlers have simply scratched the surface in their exploration of the Cape's alpine rivers. There are numerous runs with gradients exceeding 60 and 70 m/km which, when full, will surely attract the leading kayakers of the future. Paddlers such as Bruce Yelland and Phil Lloyd have certainly "pushed the grade" of rivers up a notch with runs such as the notorious Elandspad.
Cape rivers will be the testing grounds for future white water paddlers. Rivers that were once considered impossible have now been conquered and paddlers seek more difficult challenges. As equipment, skills and attitudes advance, so more rivers become possible to paddle.

The Orange River
As the largest and longest river in South Africa, the Orange provides thousands of kilometres of canoeing water. Rising to the west of the Drakensberg escarpment, it meanders through Lesotho and across the northern Cape, providing water gathered in the mountains to a semi-desert region.
The furthest up that the river has been paddled to date is from Mokhotlong in Lesotho. Known as the Sinqu in its upper reaches, the river has an altitude of 2 000 m and yet despite this, it is relatively flat.
It winds its way through the high mountains but never really drops steeply, making it suitable for expedition-type canoeing where paddlers with little river experience could cope easily with the few small rapids. The river should be paddled full in order that one be carried along fast, as several days of hard paddling are needed to cover the 300-odd kilometres through Lesotho.
Lacking in rapids and virtually devoid of vegetation and firewood, the Sinqu does not provide the idyllic tripping conditions of rivers like the Tugela, but it is still worth seeing for the massive sandstone cliffs

and formations that rise above it in places.

It was here near Mokhotlong that Reg Pearse became the first man to film the famed lammergeier, nesting in the cliffs. The river flows through sandstone gorges with the peaks of the Drakensberg standing majestically in the distance.

I do not know what effect the Lesotho Highlands water scheme will have on the river but paddlers who wish to see the gorges before they are affected by the project should consider visiting them now. One positive aspect of the project for canoeists could be the construction of roads and access to the tributaries of the Sinqu. Flowing through the Maluti Mountains, many of these rivers are steep and possibly ideal for white water canoeing.

The plains rivers in the central part of South Africa are being paddled and explored at an ever-increasing rate. The Orange — with its massive volume and diversity of landscapes — has much to offer, from flat water tripping to heavy white water.

The Orange Gorge, in the rocky wastes of the Namib, spews forth the only water to be found in hundreds of kilometres. It consists of an 18 km long bend in the river near the town of Onseepkans. The water tears through, forming rapids of grade 3 and 4, ending in the !Gariep Falls.

The Gorge is run by commercial kayaking and rafting companies and this is decidedly the best way to get to see the river on a first attempt.

More leisurely river trips on the calmer sections of the Orange are also run by commercial companies. Some use open Canadian canoes, ideal for canoe camping on the calm river. One of the attractions of the Orange for tripping lies in its exotic nature. An exotic river is one that rises in a high rainfall region and then flows through a desert. Canoeists are able to enjoy full rivers without accompanying discomfort of rain, and this has pushed the Orange to the top of the popularity stakes in canoe camping.

Various tributaries such as the Caledon and Vaal are also highly suitable canoeing rivers. As more paddlers seek new canoeing waters, it is likely that the rivers of the interior plateau will yield exciting new prospects.

Transkei

The topography of the Transkei is very similar to that of Natal. It is an area which also gets good summer rains so its rivers are ideally suited to canoeing. The Umzimvubu, which flows into the Indian Ocean at Port St Johns, is the third largest river in the country after the Orange and the Tugela. A long and lonely trip can be made from the N2 to the sea. Many grade 3 rapids and two waterfalls occur, one of which is spectacularly high. Much of the river is broad and open, but a long gorge section provides continuous rapids for at least a day.

Tributaries of the Umzimvubu such as the Tina are also large enough to paddle when flowing well in summer. The tripper on the Tina is rewarded by a view of the Tina Falls, a spectacular geological phenomenon where an incised meander has been cut off, with the river plunging through the narrow neck.

The Kei, western boundary of Transkei, is also a suitable canoeing river and is now the venue of a long distance marathon. The Umtamvuna, best known for its beautiful lagoon at Port Edward, forms the Transkei's eastern border. It flows through a deep and wooded gorge typical of the Transkei wild coast. Much of the lower section is in the Natal Parks Board reserve, so wildlife abounds and the valley is uninhabited by man. An ideal two-day trip exists from Izingolweni to the mouth. Rather rocky and steep, it can be hard on a boat, but it provides some excellent white water.

10 WHITE WATER TRIPPING

You squeeze into your kayak and lock your knees under the deck with feet pressed firmly on the footrest. The moulded seat grips you in position with back-strap and hip-pads wedging you in so that not even the roughest water can tear you from your boat. You stretch the neoprene spray cover onto the cockpit lip, grab the paddle and launch off into the swiftly flowing current.

Being "worn" so tightly, your kayak responds immediately to any movement of the paddle. In such a secure position you feel confident despite the booming sound of a massive rapid ahead. Sealed inside the boat you can be completely submerged or capsized and spring back up to the surface. A quick Eskimo roll has you upright and you are carried on again, relentlessly forward.

As you paddle down a deep rapid, you spin around and drift backwards into a massive standing wave. Now stationary, you surf as the water rushes by, turning sideways, left and right, even spinning through 360 degrees. The tricks you can do are numerous and eventually to exit the wave you paddle forward and dip your nose into the current. It is immediately pushed beneath you as you loop into the air and flop back into the water, drifting off again downstream.

Rough water canoeing has been virtually revolutionised by polyethylene kayaks. Their indestructibility has made previously uncanoeable waters a distinct possibility. They are also extremely forgiving, so that a situation which would break a glassfibre canoe in two is no more than an anxious moment in plastic.

Of course glassfibre canoes still have their value and can be used quite successfully for wild water, but very rocky rivers should be avoided and a patching kit needs to be taken along.

Rivers suitable for white water canoeing fall between two extremes: the large-volume rivers which carry massive quantities of water through major valleys to the sea, and the mountain torrents which rush through steep, narrow gorges. Typical of the former type are rivers such as the Colorado in the Grand Canyon, USA, and the Zambezi below Victoria Falls. Mountain streams are numerous and nerve-racking and should be tackled only by experienced wild water paddlers. The wild water paddled in South Africa is seldom either of these, usually fitting somewhere in between the two extremes.

Paddling on the mature, wide rivers gives one an awe-inspiring sense of their power. The swiftly moving mass of water picks up a canoe like a twig and flings it mercilessly along. Large, standing waves tower above you as you tumble into the massive holes and feel the full force of the river. Menacing brown eddies surge and boil on either side of the main current, occasionally snatching a boat and pulling it down into the murky depths. The more daring paddlers on the Zambezi paddle voluntarily into these surging whirlpools to be sucked out of sight and spat out at some other point a few seconds later.

Such large rivers are few in South Africa, with the Orange, Tugela and Umkomaas being the best of them, but the summer floods in this country make many lesser rivers capable of providing the big water experience.

Steep mountainside rivers are much shallower and extremely fast flowing. Previously avoided by rough water enthusiasts, they are now being tackled with increasing regularity as the advantages of polyethylene kayaks are being fully realised.

Mountain rivers are usually found near the source so the levels rise and fall very rapidly, which means that they can be paddled only after heavy rains. The steep gradient is unrelenting, with continuous boulder fields, small waterfalls, ledges and massive rocks. Eddies to rest in are few and one has to claw oneself into them as quickly as possible. There you get a short rest and a chance to glance downstream at the next few drops and find another breakout point.

The Umkomasane River and Thrombosis Gorge on the Umzimkulu provide such mountain stream sections. Even the Ndedema Gorge in

Deepdale falls on the Umkomaas; skill and courage are put to the test. (Tim Biggs)

the Drakensberg, better known for hiking and Bushman paintings, has been paddled. There are numerous such rivers in the Natal Drakensberg and western Cape fold mountains and most of them are still to be explored. The Pholela, Loteni and Bushman's in the former range offer promising possibilities. But these rivers are for the brave experts only. Few can handle the numerous waterfalls and dangerous situations, and those who are interested in wild water would do better to stick to the larger rivers or less treacherous mountain sections until they are confident of paddling to the limits of possibility.

Waterfalls

Nothing can beat the sensation of free-falling through space and landing safely in a pool of water. There is a certain sense of ecstasy in the knowledge that one has cheated death and possesses a measure of invincibility. If one can survive such a hazard, anything seems possible. And here lies the danger.

Paddlers are divided in their opinions as to the merits of shooting waterfalls. Some feel that no skill is involved at all and that it is all left to gravity, although there is no doubt that the speed at which the kayak is travelling and the angle at which it leaves the lip of the fall determine its position on landing. It is certainly impressive to see an experienced wild water paddler landing his boat in the correct position at the right angle. Is it luck or good judgement?

Landing in the wrong place can have serious consequences. One could end up on rocks or get caught in an immense stopper. Landing at the wrong angle is likely to seriously damage one's back, so think carefully before you try to gain immortality on high falls. You might just be more mortal than you think!

Certainly high risks are involved in the shooting of waterfalls. They present their dangers, but they are there for the brave. Safety must of course play a major part in anything that presents a high level of risk. Minimise the risks by having helpers standing by with throw-lines, use the correct safety equipment and don't tackle anything you feel is beyond your capabilities.

Rapids

Wild water canoeing is all about rapids. They provide the excitement that makes river canoeing so rewarding. But rapids that are underestimated or treated with indifference tend to demonstrate their omnipotence.

An international river grading system was formulated in order to give paddlers an idea of the degree of difficulty of a rapid. This system is controversial throughout the world, as some paddlers believe that rivers are too diverse in their characteristics, degrees of difficulty and danger levels to be categorised by a simple 1 to 6 system. Paddlers might also be inclined to paddle sections of river according to their grading rather than judging the river for themselves on the day.

Wild water is wild by name and nature and defies accurate categorisation, especially in South Africa with its all-or-nothing rainfall pattern. Levels can change dramatically, and a river that is little more than a dry bed at one moment, can become a raging torrent the next. It is for this reason that South African rivers have flowed ungraded for such a long time, although moves are now afoot to introduce grading and give the paddler some idea of a river's difficulty, taking medium summer flow as the norm. But as flows change continuously, the river grading system must be treated with circumspection.

The following six categories are included in the international system:

Grade 1 — Not Difficult
The river is flowing, but there are only small, shallow sand banks with a few rocks strewn on them.

Grade 1: Nanette Rennie weaves her way through the rocks of the Umgeni. (Alick Rennie)

Grade 2 — Moderately difficult
The way down the river is clear but simple obstructions exist. Small stoppers and small drops may be present. There are places where the current accelerates.

Grade 2: A K2 in a small rapid of the Umkomaas. (Alick Rennie)

Grade 3 — Difficult
There is a good route down the rapid which can be seen from the kayak. Waves are high and irregular. Boulders and obstructions may be numerous. Stoppers and small eddies exist.

Grade 3: Skirting large stoppers on a full Umkomaas. (Alick Rennie)

Grade 4: Jerome Truran in the turbulent waters of a gorge on the Buffalo River. (Alick Rennie)

Grade 4 — Very difficult
The route is not always clear. Most paddlers choose to inspect the rapid from the bank before shooting. Rapids are continuous and the water is heavy. Stoppers are powerful. The paddler is required to manoeuvre continually.

Grade 5 — Extremely difficult
Inspection from the bank is essential because serious dangers exist in the rapid. The paddling is continuously difficult, with large drops, narrow passages, very complex boulder fields and difficult holes.

Grade 5: Alick Rennie is pounded by heavy waves in Island rapid in the flooding Umgeni. (Rowan Sampson)

Grade 6 — The absolute limit
All the dangers of white water exist to the utmost degree, and water level is critical to permit paddling. The consequences of a mistake are extremely serious. One cannot attempt such a rapid without acknowledging that one is risking one's life.

Grade 6: Thrombosis gorge on the Umzimkulu in flood; suicidal at this level. (Tim Biggs)

There is talk of adding a seventh grade to this scale to cater for the rise in standards and aspirations of the modern white water paddler.

This grading system is applied in particular in Europe where numerous river guide books are available. River sections are graded 2, 3 or 4 for example, and difficult rapids within these sections are indexed, so that a section rated as 2.4 indicates a section of grade 2 river with a grade 4 rapid on it.

This system might yet be applied in South Africa, with guide books available on the major white water rivers. But until it is, paddlers will have to do their own grading and decide for themselves on their own capabilities. Perhaps, after all, this is the best way of classifying the difficulty of a river.

11 CANOEING TRIATHLONS

When Tim Cornish sprang from his canoe after more than two hours of canoeing on Hartbeespoort Dam to set off on the 90 km cycle ride to Pretoria, few believed that he could keep going at the cracking pace he was setting. It is now history that he did, as well as running 42 km to Sandton after that.

That was 1983 and although many other exceptional endurance performances had occurred before and have occurred since, Cornish's uncanny ability to race this triathlon the first time it was held as though he had done it many times before, made it all the more remarkable. What generated so much interest in this first triathlon was that sportsmen were entering the realm of the unknown. Could athletes keep going for nine hours without collapsing from exhaustion? How would changing from one form of sport to the next affect them? Would it be a help or a hindrance?

This triple fitness activity has challenged and united canoeists, cyclists, runners and swimmers from all over the world. Essentially a combination of swimming, cycling and running, the canoe, cycle, run triathlon is a popular form in this country. The Leppin Iron Man remains the premier canoe triathlon event, but numerous other shorter races are held throughout the country.

Provincial and national championships are raced over fixed distances, the standard event being an 8 km paddle, 40 km cycle and 10 km run. The "half standard" consists of a 4 km paddle, 20 km cycle and 5 km run. The events of the early eighties were held over differing distances, with the lie of the land and distances from dams to suitable finishing points deciding the lengths of the stages. These races were more popular with canoeists than the standard distances for they usually had a greater ratio of canoeing to cycling and running than the standard distance events.

The triathlon is one of the most gruelling long distance events and is widely recognised as the ultimate test of aerobic conditioning. Like the Duzi marathon, it favours the canoeing runner. The addition of cycling creates interest and difficulty, for the athlete has to master and train for yet another demanding sport.

For the working man to find sufficient hours in the day to train towards peak fitness in three sports is virtually impossible. You have to work out a training schedule that will best suit your lifestyle and abilities. Roughly 14 hours' training a week are needed for anyone who hopes to finish the Leppin Iron Man in reasonable condition.

Weekly training

A good weekly programme would include:

Canoeing
Five sessions:
- Three one-and-a-quarter-hour sessions at medium pace.
- One two-hour session at medium pace.
- One one-hour fast session with sprints included.

Hard sessions should be alternated with easier sessions. For example, if you do a short, hard paddle on a Tuesday, Wednesday's paddle should be medium paced. Thursday's session is then a two-hour paddle and Friday's is easy.

Cycling
Four rides:
- Two short, hard rides just over one hour long.
- Two long rides, one of two hours and one of three hours.

This would give you seven hours or 200 km of cycling per week.

Running
Four runs:
- Two of 12 km at medium pace
- One of 21 km slowly
- One of 8 km fast.

This would total about 50 to 60 km, the equivalent of four hours of training.

Such a training schedule suits me, but it might be totally unsuited to other triathletes. As a relatively new sport, triathlon training is still at the developmental stage. You might do best to work out your own schedule according to your weaknesses and strengths.

Triathletes who are strong on running, for example, might cut down on this and do more canoeing and cycling. Cycling and running are inclined to complement each other, so time spent on the bike helps improve your running. Canoeing is the odd one out and needs to be worked on slightly more than the other two activities.

This programme means training twice a day six days a week with a single session on the seventh day. Obviously such a programme is difficult to adhere to, but it is good to have a difficult target so that if you break, you are still getting in good training. If you have an easy programme that you break from, then you are undertraining, which will not be beneficial.

One of the dangers of training hard is overtraining. This can usually be avoided by having long rest periods between hard sessions. If you start to feel tired continuously and are unable to train properly because of tiredness, it is time to cut back and skip a few sessions. You will find that the rest revitalises you and you will start going better than before. It is this kind of rest that is needed before a race. Several days of slow training or none at all will ensure that you do not start a race tired.

The long-term training scheme

More important than the weekly programme is the long-term training scheme. To reach peak fitness for an ultra distance event, one needs to work at it for several months, and each season's training helps in the following season. Eventually one undergoes a physical metamorphosis and becomes a super-tuned triathlete.

The ultra distance triathlete should work at 10 long training sessions in each sport within a season. This would mean 10 paddling sessions in excess of two hours, 10 100 km cycle rides and 10 runs of 25 to 30 km. Include races in this plan. This gives a solid stamina base and introduces the triathlete to the physical and mental stress of long distances.

Also important in the long-term training schedule is the combination training session. Either two or three of the activities can be combined to give the triathlete the experience of changing from one form of exercise to the next.

No change-over is easy. Your legs lie idle in the canoe, while your arms are hard at work. When you leave the water to start cycling, you find very stubborn, sore legs that need to be warmed up. Running is also sufficiently different from cycling for it to feel awkward for the first one or two kilometres.

Always start the next stage relatively slowly so that your limbs have sufficient time to warm up before you start turning on the pace.

There is no doubt that triathloning is to the detriment of canoeing form in the short term. No athlete, no matter how good he is, can remain on top for canoeing while 66 per cent of his training time is spent running and cycling. For this reason the triathlete canoeist must work out his training schedule very carefully, making sure that the major canoeing, running and triathlon races which he plans to enter are at different times of the year.

A good way for the ultra distance athlete to plan his year would be to start with the Duzi in January, then add cycling for the Iron Man Canoe Triathlon in February and finally work on running for the Comrades in May. In this way he would be building on fitness from the previous event and dropping those activities that are no longer needed.

12 SURF AND SEA

Sea canoeing in South Africa takes on two forms: surfing and off-shore paddling. Our coastline offers numerous beaches with warm waters, ideal for surfing and setting out to sea. Although the seas are rough, the weather is often warm and windless so sometimes easy conditions prevail. This makes sea canoeing a pleasant and exciting experience, even for the less experienced and cautious mariner. Off-shore paddling is a risky business, however, for those not acquainted with the sea. It is best to start by playing in the surf and only paddle out to sea under the guidance of experienced ski paddlers.

Skis are used more frequently than kayaks for both surfing and off-shore paddling, although the tupperware canoe has become popular in the surf. Off-shore paddling and surfing are markedly different activities, demanding different skills and providing totally different experiences.

The surf paddler's art resembles that of the surf boarder crossed with that of the wild water canoeist, while the long distance off-shore racer needs the skill of the ocean yachtsman combined with great stamina and fitness.

Surfing

Few forms of canoeing can beat surfing for sheer enjoyment. A ski on a wave can travel up to 30 km per hour; it is exceptionally manoeuvrable and is capable of some fantastic acrobatics. It can be spun through 360 degrees while on a wave, looped end over end and popped out of the water clear of the surface. The Eskimo roll is, needless to say, an essential part of surfing, for one does not stay upright for long in heavy surf.

One sits on rather than in a ski. It is a short, flat, surfboard-like craft with a hollowed out seat and footrests. Straps across the feet and a seatbelt across the paddler's waist hold him in place when capsized. It is impossible to roll a ski without a belt. This is joined by a strip of Velcro material which comes apart easily if the paddler's roll fails.

The low back deck of a ski makes it an exceptionally easy craft to roll. By lying backwards, one is able to get one's centre of gravity so low that all that is needed to right the boat is a flick of the hips. The sea can also help one upright as waves fling the capsized ski about.

Surfing manoeuvres on a ski resemble the movements made on a surfboard. In fact surfing has developed so fast in the last few years that the ski paddler's art is now markedly different from that of other canoeists. He is able to control his craft precisely in massive surf, doing manoeuvres that the average canoeist does not even know exist. For this reason the serious surfer is a specialist and seldom takes part in other forms of canoeing.

The average canoeist without this specialist skill can still enjoy the surf in his own way. Besides riding waves, paddlers can enjoy nose dives, pop-outs and loops. Heavy surf resembles rough water and is in fact a good training ground for the white water canoeist. Canoeists preparing for trips on the Zambezi Gorge below Victoria Falls, or for the Colorado Grand Canyon use heavy surf to become acquainted with powerful waves. After a tumble in a large wave, the paddler is forced to roll up, but he faces no danger from submerged rocks as he would in a river. This makes the surf one of the best places to practise rolling.

A short boat in heavy surf is flung about continuously so simply being out there and leaving everything else to the sea creates interesting possibilities. There is nothing that so accurately resembles the action of a washing machine as paddling in the surf.

A paddler in action in the surf. (Photographer unknown)

Off-shore paddling

The long paddle-ski is an exceptionally seaworthy boat. Experienced paddlers do not have to avoid rough conditions, but rather seek them out for the excitement they provide. Off-shore paddling is predominantly a competitive sport, with the four-day run from Port Elizabeth to East London the most gruelling and prestigious in the country. But several long sea trips bear testimony to the interest shown in sea canoeing for the sake of the pleasure of the sea.

Tony Scott and Paul Chalupsky made history in 1979 by paddling from Cape Town to Durban in order to raise funds for life-saving. Since then the entire South African coast from Oranjemund to Kosi Bay has been paddled. Canoeing Springbok Mat Carlisle showed the adaptability of these boats by using one for fishing and becoming a highly successful deep-sea fisherman. Several other intrepid paddlers are now following his example.

This country has had its fair share of world-class long distance ski paddlers, of whom Oscar Chalupsky is perhaps the most successful. Besides numerous local victories, he has won the Molokai event in Hawaii several times, a race that is regarded as the unofficial world championship.

Paddling of kayaks at sea is limited off our shores owing to the danger of a capsize and the continuous taking in of water, but in many parts kayaks are used most successfully. South Africans Sean Rice and Colin Simpkins made canoeing history by setting the English Channel crossing record in a K2 canoe, which is an indication of the high standard of sea paddling in this country despite, or perhaps because of, the harsh conditions experienced. The open sea is cut off from the land by huge pounding surf and anyone who wishes to paddle off-shore must first be able to negotiate it. The waters are infested with sharks, and although I have never heard of a paddler being attacked, shark phobia persists in most of our minds. The coastline also lacks natural and sheltered inlets which would provide protection from the huge rollers of the open sea.

All this has led to a select and hardy breed of paddler who revels in these rough conditions, but for the less daring there are still suitable forms of off-shore paddling. The weather is often calm and warm, making the surf and open sea fairly hospitable. Certain sheltered beaches offer easy launches and shark nets set the mind at ease. The Durban beachfront and some of the South coast beaches in Natal offer easy sections for paddling out at sea.

13 SAFETY

Canoeing is a relatively safe sport, providing high excitement and tension at a relatively low danger level. If one does capsize, swimming in large rapids with a life-jacket and helmet on is much safer than it feels. Nevertheless, the object of every canoeist should be to make canoeing even safer than it is already. This can only be done if canoeists take the necessary precautions, wear the correct safety gear and keep a lookout for fellow paddlers in trouble. It is all too easy to paddle past a canoeist in difficulty when the heat of a race is on. It is also difficult to tell when a situation is becoming critical and a fellow paddler needs help.

Every paddler has a responsibility to stay out of trouble, for it is not

Lorna Oliver takes the steps on the Ernie Pearce weir. Steps do away with the steep angle and stopper, characteristic problems associated with weirs. (John Oliver)

Herve de Rauville sinks into the stopper of the Albert Falls weir before bouncing safely back onto the surface. (Val Adamson)

only one's own life that one puts at risk, but also the lives of the rescuers. Wear a life-jacket and helmet in all but the calmest rivers. Paddle with a group, especially with paddlers who are experienced and know the river. If your whole party is new to the section you are paddling, approach every rapid with caution. If you cannot see a breakout point in the rapid ahead of you, get out and scout from the bank. There is always a chance that rapids shot "blind" may end up in waterfalls or trees.

The South African Canoe Federation is at present involved in grading rivers and paddlers, after which a canoeist will only be allowed to paddle on a certain section of river if his grading is sufficiently high. Such impositions are necessary if paddlers take chances with their own lives and those of others, but self-discipline is perhaps the most sensible way of approaching canoeing safety. Know your capabilities and do not overextend yourself. If you wish to shoot a grade 5 rapid, develop your skills accordingly. A runner who wishes to cover 10 km in 30 minutes cannot start fast and hope to last the distance. Using such a method he would obviously fail; so will the over-ambitious canoeist, but failing in a grade 5 rapid has far more serious consequences than failing at a target time in running. A runner trains for months until he feels sufficiently fit to tackle his task. The same applies to the rough water canoeist. There is no substitute for time spent on the water. The more experience the canoeist has on the river, the safer and more proficient he becomes.

Dangerous situations

Man-made obstacles
Perhaps the words of iron man Eddie King best sum up the effect of man's intrusion on the flow of rivers. "As long as you challenge the forces of nature in a pure unadulterated state and you treat her with sufficient respect, things will be alright. In a virginal state the natural tendency of any river will be to spit you out on the side. But when man starts building weirs and cable and causeways and irrigation dams and pipes across rivers, they become lethal."

Man-made obstacles restrict the natural flow of water and objects such as canoes and canoeists are easily trapped. Concrete blocks and reinforcing rods sometimes remain in the river, providing lethal debris.

Weirs
These often innocuous-looking man-made drops are some of the most deadly obstacles found in river canoeing. They occur regularly and provide canoeists with some exciting white water, but their dangers are often ignored. Besides the possibility of loose concrete blocks and shallow submerged rocks immediately below the weir, the stopper wave, if large enough, can trap a canoe and paddler.

Always check up on the stopper and pull back before shooting a weir. Make sure you can get out of it if you capsize. Find the deepest spot below the weir. Full, high-volume weirs require a high-speed negotiation in order to clear the stopper, while shallow rocky weirs should be shot slowly so as to avoid hitting the rocks below with force and breaking the nose of your canoe.

Some weirs such as the Cradock Weir on the Fish and the Duzi Bridge Weir are best shot semi-sideways as this saves the nose from the rocks below. But a weir with a powerful stopper should always be shot straight, as a sideways shoot dumps a canoe right into the stopper wave. It is virtually impossible to extricate oneself from such a position without capsizing.

Low-level bridges
The Lowveld Crocodile in the eastern Transvaal is notorious for its low-level bridges. Jerome Truran and other skilled paddlers capsize to fit under them and roll up on the other side, thus avoiding a portage. This of course has its dangers as submerged trees trapped under such bridges could in turn trap the paddler, but paddlers who do such things do a thorough check beforehand and then keep the situation under control.

Low-level bridges are particularly dangerous to paddlers who do not understand them and approach too near on the upstream side. The current can very quickly suck a boat under, wrapping it around a pillar or trapping both boat and paddler beneath the bridge.

Many low-level bridges can be negotiated by ducking your head in

Safety 159

A paddler keeps his head down to squeeze under a low-level bridge. (Alick Rennie)

order to fit under them. If you do not duck low enough, you can get a pretty hard knock on the head! It is worth practising to see how low you can go. It might just save you a severe headache or a time-consuming portage.

Cables and wires
Cables and wires are usually found only where man is working in the river, where bridges are being constructed or sand is being dredged. They are sometimes the remains of slalom courses or swingbridges.

Look for the point in the river where the cable is at its highest. This is usually close to the bank. Capsize if necessary, but if the wire hits you, try to flick it over your head.

A cable used to stretch across the Umkomaas River just above Number 7 Rapid where the water flows extremely fast. In such a case, it would be sensible to capsize to get under rather than hit the cable at high speed.

Canoe congestion
In popular races like the Duzi, safe rivers are made dangerous when too many canoes enter a rapid at the same time. Develop your skills so that you become good enough to leave the masses behind, but if this is not possible, rely on your ingenuity.

Do not be put off by the boats around you. Give the person in front of you sufficient room so that if he fouls it up, you do not become part of his log-jam.

If you should fall out in front of a large group, straighten your boat up immediately so that several people do not paddle straight through it. Get out of the main current so that you are out of the way of the boats behind you. This should save you from having your boat chopped in half or being seriously injured by having a canoe bash into you. Remember that the boats behind you cannot stop in a fast-flowing current so it is up to you to get out of their way. The best way of looking after your own interests is to look after the interests of the people around you. Forgetting about other canoeing traffic is like forgetting about other traffic on the highway.

The better you are, the better the canoeists around you are likely to be. One often finds that the front group in a race tears down rapids without mishap, while further back a novice falls out, blocking the river and causing several boats to build up in a log-jam.

Natural obstacles

The most perilous natural obstacles found in rivers must be **trees**. The branches spread like talons into a strong current, sieving the water and catching solid obstacles which become pinned against them. The current holds them there with terrific force, and a trapped canoe can seldom be extricated from tree branches.

It is therefore imperative that a canoeist keeps well clear of trees. I have always maintained that a flat but strong-flowing river continuous-

The sit and wait game of canoe congestion. Don't tolerate queue jumpers. (Val Adamson)

Safety 161

Rowan Sampson at play in a stopper on the Umkomaas. What's fun to him is a load of trouble to lesser paddlers. (Alick Rennie)

ly blocked with trees is more dangerous than a huge raging torrent. What makes it even more treacherous is the fact that people are often unaware of its dangers.

Small flooding rivers are particularly hazardous with regard to trees. The branches reach from bank to bank, and drifting logs become jammed across the stream. Any river which appears likely to have tree blocks in it should always be scouted from the bank before being paddled.

Overhanging rocks seldom occur in a river. I have only seen them in the sandstone of the Drakensberg streams. The water flows underneath them, much the same as down a plug-hole. Mountain white water paddlers need to look out for them. They are commonest on the outside of bends as the water undercuts the bank, wearing the lower part away.

Stoppers which form naturally in the river, often at the bottom of ledges, are not as dangerous as those found at weirs. A rock ledge seldom spans the entire width of a river, so the stopper presents a shoot at either end or somewhere along its length where a paddler can paddle through. If you are caught in a stopper, you can work your way towards the shoot and get washed out. Alternatively, by capsizing — whether by accident or plan — one can be washed out of the stopper by the current flowing downstream underneath.

The better paddlers loop out of stoppers. As the nose digs into the water flowing downstream, the boat stands on its end. It is shot out of the water and hopefully out of reach of the stopper. Such a manoeuvre is known as an "ender" and is considered a macho move by rough water "turkeys". The ender is also done as one of the dance steps or fun manoeuvres in white water canoeing.

Being **pinned in a kayak** against a rock can have terrible consequences. The indestructibility of a plastic canoe can have its drawbacks, the most serious being that if you are in the boat when it is trapped on a rock, you cannot break the deck to get out. The slightly larger cockpits that are found on the later designs make them much safer as the paddler can release his knees from under the deck and swim free.

Paddling in a group also helps avoid a paddler becoming trapped in his boat, for friends with throw bags and courage can get a paddler out of almost any situation. I have often heard stories of paddlers who would have drowned if it had not been for another paddler coming to the rescue. I have seldom heard of canoeists drowning, especially when in the company of other canoeists.

Figure 13.1 Ways of escaping from a stopper

(a) Normal exit: Brace and paddle to side of stopper. By pushing nose into flow you will be washed out.

(b) Capsize and roll out: Hanging upside-down in the water will create enough drag to take you clear.

(c) Sky rocketing out (similar to an ender except tail of boat rather than nose is dipped into current).

Equipment

The life-jacket and helmet have already been discussed in Chapter 1. Suffice it to say that the **life-jacket** is perhaps the most valuable item in the paddler's assortment of gear. It provides him with buoyancy whilst swimming, and padding which protects him from bruising on the rocks. A paddler who overturns in shallow water is dragged along the bottom of the river, bumping against rocks until he is able to roll upright or extricate himself from his boat. A well-padded, experienced canoeist will tolerate the bashing in absolute calm, knowing that a full helmet and life-jacket will protect him until he finds the opportunity to roll.

The type of **helmet** used is important. Rocks usually hit the paddler on the side of the head so helmets should obviously not leave the ears exposed. Forehead and temples should also be protected, so a full helmet made of a strong material such as polypropylene is more of a necessity than a luxury for the serious white water canoeist.

Buoyancy, also referred to as flotation, in the canoe is important not only for the sake of the canoe, but also for the paddler. If you fall out, you will be able to keep afloat by hanging onto the canoe. Buoyancy is obtained by cutting polystyrene or closed-cell foam to fit in both ends of the canoe. It is of little use to have buoyancy in one end of the canoe only, for if you fall out the canoe will float vertically with one end pointing straight downwards, bashing itself to bits on the bed of the river.

Plastic soccer balls and beach balls can be used for flotation, but they have a tendency to float out once the canoe is swamped and do no more than pollute the river. Make sure they are tied securely in the boat.

Throw ropes or **throw bags** are new items of equipment available to rough water paddlers. The throw bag consists of 15 to 25 m of floating rope folded into a bag which can be thrown to a paddler in distress.

The bag should be thrown into the water upstream of the paddler so that it can float down to him. If it is folded and used correctly it can be used immediately and may mean the difference between life and death.

Throw bags are used extensively in certain countries overseas, but I have seldom seen one used in South Africa. Accidents happen fairly fast, leaving little time for helpers to get out rescue equipment such as ropes. Usually paddlers are washed free or can be reached by other canoeists, but throw ropes should be considered by paddlers tackling extreme white water sections.

Warm clothing is particularly important in cold water and winter conditions, for hypothermia is a killer and one of the greatest dangers facing paddlers in colder climes. Fortunately most South African canoeing is done in the luke-warm waters of summer, so cold presents no problem. The winter rainfall region, however, demands warm clothing at times. Special paddling anoraks, long-sleeved T-shirts or wetsuits need to be worn.

Thermal underwear like the ever-popular "hally hanson" vests and T-shirts provide sufficient warmth for most canoeing in this country.

What can go wrong?

In any sport with an element of danger, things can go wrong. Accidents that can happen include:
- capsizing and having to swim in a rapid.
- a swimmer being held in a stopper.
- the kayak becoming trapped and the paddler being unable to exit.
- various other accidents and injuries, a dislocated shoulder being the most common.

Swimming in a rapid

All paddlers experience this unpleasant aspect of the sport at some time or another. The answer is not to panic and to do what you can to protect yourself and your boat from damage.

By hanging onto your boat, you provide yourself with buoyancy while keeping the boat straight and minimising the chance of damage to it. Lie on your back and hold the boat by the stern, keeping it straight with the current. Use your feet to push away from rocks. Once you are through the rapid, swim to the bank using a life-saver-type kick and the ferry glide on the boat.

If possible, hang onto your paddle and boat. The only time to leave them is when hanging on would be dangerous. The boat should be held upright so that no damage is done to the deck and cockpits by rocks.

Good swimming technique: this paddler has a firm grip on his paddle and the tail of his boat. He must now keep his boat straight with the current to avoid having it wrapped around a rock. (Val Adamson)

In a large-volume river such as the Tugela in flood, one can do little to get the boat to the bank in large rapids. Leave it if you are losing and run like hell in the hopes of picking it up in one piece below the rapids. There are obvious advantages to having a boat packed with buoyancy.

Being held in a stopper

In the case of a swimmer being held in a stopper he should be thrown a throw-bag in order to be pulled out. None but the biggest waves will hold a swimmer as legs dangling downwards help to get one washed out.

A canoe on a rope can also be floated into the stopper from above in order to give the paddler something to hold onto so he can be pulled to the edge. This should be done in extreme cases only as the swimmer can be hit by the boat. It also takes a long time to sort this out and it is usually sufficient to throw a rope.

I have heard it said that taking one's life-jacket off and swimming down into the current is a good way of getting out of a stopper. This, I think, is a good theory only. One is likely to need a life-jacket once out of the stopper and it is better to stay on the surface and work one's way to the side than submerge into the murky depths in the hopes of popping up later. A very strong current is quite capable of sinking a paddler in any life-jacket and washing him free in it, and a swimmer in distress cannot fiddle with zips and ties in order to release his life-jacket.

It is usually a kayak with a paddler still intact that becomes trapped as it floats high on the surface where all the water is flowing upstream, See **Stoppers** on p. 161 for tips on how to get out. Use falling out as a last resort. This, of course, happens without much trying.

Being trapped in a kayak

(See information on the kayak on p. 162)

Injuries

One of the advantages of canoeing is that there are very few related injuries. **Painful wrists**, developed from overtraining, are best cured by rest. If this develops during a multi-day marathon, strapping the wrist tightly should make the pain tolerable for the rest of the race.

Perhaps the most severe and common injury for rough water paddlers is the **dislocated shoulder.** This usually occurs when either arm is positioned above and behind the head or when the paddler is bracing across a hole or a stopper and is suddenly capsized. The paddle hitting the bottom or even the force of the water can be enough to shoot the top of the upper arm out of the socket.

The paddler should develop a style where strokes using the arm held high above and behind the head are unnecessary. Such strokes are inefficient; the paddle should always be held in front of the paddler.

A canoeist with a dislocated shoulder finds paddling and swimming virtually impossible. Needless to say, this could have serious consequences, especially as a shoulder is more likely to dislocate in rough water where one needs to be able to swim rather efficiently.

Most dislocations are extremely painful and prevent further paddling. Relocating the arm is also difficult and painful and should be left to a doctor unless one is skilled in the operation.

Shoulder dislocation is best avoided by good rough water paddling technique. Practise the following:
- Avoid strokes where the arms are extended above and behind the head.
- Lie forward and grip the paddle against the boat when capsized and preparing to roll, otherwise it could catch on the bottom and pull on the shoulders.
- When executing the Eskimo roll, avoid getting your arms in awkward positions. The nearer you can get to having your upper arm against your side, the less likely it is to dislocate. Any paddler with a good rolling technique is extremely unlikely to dislocate a shoulder whilst rolling. It is only the previously dislocated shoulder that redislocates when the forces against it are mild.

A paddler takes off over the lip of a waterfall. (Alick Rennie)

A free fall into the turbulence below. (Alick Rennie)
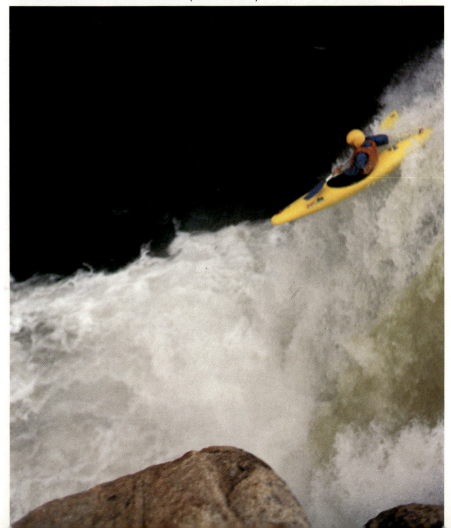

Tim Biggs sets off down a grade six rapid on the Dwars River in the Western Cape. (Richard Smithers)

He is spun around on the lip of the falls . . . (Richard Smithers)

washed over . . . (Richard Smithers)

. . . and heads for the plunge pool. He emerged unscathed. (Richard Smithers)

The Deepdale falls on the Umkomaas. Not only the height but the massive volume of this river makes it one of the most impressive falls regularly shot. (Alick Rennie)

A surfer does a bottom turn and shoots off to the point of greatest energy on the wave. (Photographer unknown)

14 HEALTH

All sport should do something to improve an athlete's health and canoeing is no exception. This is certainly the case in most instances, but there are certain conditions where any sport can have a detrimental effect on the sportsman's well-being. The long distance nature of South African canoeing and the possibility of waterborne diseases present the paddler with certain health hazards.

Dehydration

As most — if not all — rivers in South Africa have undrinkable water, the paddler needs to carry his fluid supply with him. This can be done, but dehydration remains a serious and at times neglected problem for canoeists. Once dehydration sets in, performance is significantly affected and the canoeist may be at risk of developing heat stroke. Symptoms of dehydration include weakness, fatigue, light-headedness and cramps. Urine output decreases significantly.

Prevent dehydration by taking the following precautions:
- Pre-race loading: aim to drink up to 500 ml in the hour preceding the race.
- Start drinking *early* and aim to drink between 500 and 1 000 ml per hour. The volume of fluids taken in will vary with the environmental temperature and duration of the race.
- Reasonably diluted urine should be passed within two hours of starting an event.
- Diarrhoea and vomiting will significantly increase the chances of becoming dehydrated.
- Salt tablets do *not* have a place in the treatment of dehydration.

Once dehydration exists, the paddler should *stop or slow down* sufficiently to drink enough to correct the problem, that is until diluted urine is passed or the symptoms improve significantly.

Hypoglycaemia

This is the medical term for low blood sugar. Canoeists who compete in long (four to six hour) events without access to any nourishment may feel light-headed, dizzy, very weak and sweaty and have impaired vision. These symptoms of low blood sugar may be prevented or cured by the ingestion of chocolate, glucose, sweets or 250 to 500 ml of Coke or another cool drink.

Injuries

Canoeists who sustain cuts and lacerations must remember to have a booster of 0,5 ml of tetanus toxoid if they have not received tetanus immunisation in the preceding four years. Don't be content to put on some antiseptic ointment and leave it at that.

Bilharzia

Most east-flowing rivers, especially those nearer the coast, are infected with the main bilharzial parasites, *Schistosoma haematobium* and *S. mansoni*.

The cercarial larvae which infect man are released from snails which are more prevalent at the slow-flowing banks of rivers and edges of dams. The larvae, which cannot be seen with the naked eye, penetrate the wet skin of man and some *itching* may be experienced. A latent period of about four weeks may be followed by a short *flu-like* illness with a high fever, body aches and pains, weakness and headache. This occurs when the eggs are being laid in the host's tissues.

Thereafter what happens is dependent on the extent of the infection and the development of immunity. Chronic bilharzia has many vague symptoms of which fatigue, lethargy and weakness are the most predominant. Weight loss, anaemia and blood-stained urine may set in from six to eight weeks after exposure.

Guidelines for management
- Keep exposure to infected water to a minimum; avoid swimming in the river after the event.
- Showering and vigorous rubbing with a towel soon after exposure may help to decrease larval penetration.
- It is *not* recommended to take bilharzia treatment medication prior to an event to try to "prevent" bilharzia from developing.
- Canoeists who are *completely well* after contact with water and only have a positive blood test should *not* have treatment.
- If you suspect bilharzia consult your general practitioner who will attempt to prove or disprove the diagnosis with a urine and blood test and prescribe treatment as indicated.

Sun protection

Sunburn is one of the more serious and neglected hazards of canoeing. The effects of sunburn are usually only problematic several years after exposure, and consequently canoeists are not aware of the harm being done until it is too late. One should always use a waterproof sun protection ointment, and also apply it in slightly overcast conditions. An ointment with a protection factor of at least six should be applied.

Diarrhoea

Diarrhoea and dysenteric illnesses may be a problem for canoeists who are particularly at risk as a result of swallowing bacterially contaminated water, having to change their diet, or simply as a result of increased physical activity.
Important points to remember are:
- Diarrhoea greatly increases the chances of becoming dehydrated, so if you develop diarrhoea your fluid intake must increase significantly.
- Diarrhoea associated with a high fever and/or shivering attacks may indicate a dysenteric illness, and medical attention should be obtained as soon as possible.
- Simple "dietary" or exercise-induced diarrhoea is usually self-limiting and will respond rapidly to anti-diarrhoea medication. There are several highly effective brands that may be obtained from a chemist without a doctor's prescription.

Canoeist's "sciatica"

Sitting in a canoe for hours on end, or in a seat that is especially uncomfortable, can put pressure on the sciatic nerve. This can lead to pins and needles, numb feet and legs, or "numb bum", the latter being an almost unbearable and debilitating pain. A seat that is too narrow increases the pressure on the sciatic nerve. A broad, shallow seat can help to solve the problem. Movement also helps, but this is difficult in a wobbly K1. Start early in a long race by moving around on the seat as much as you can before numbness sets in.

Foam rubber can help, but layers of it are inclined to make the seat narrower, thus increasing the problem. Test a seat in training and make continual changes until you get it right. Try several different models of seats.

Cramps

Cramps recurring during an event are frequently a manifestation of under-hydration. A frequently repeated unusual physical movement such as working a rudder pedal also precipitates cramps.

Cramps are *not* caused by a loss of salt and taking salt tablets is not recommended as a cure. Slowing down on the physical exercise and increasing your fluid intake will usually improve or cure cramps.

15 OTHER ASPECTS OF CANOEING

The environment

For the active canoeist, canoeing is a way of life. It becomes all-engrossing. Everything that happens is seen in canoeing terms. Rain at night means a full river the next day; SA Championship races in the Western Province mean a holiday in Cape Town; the Duzi just after your wedding means a honeymoon on the river.

But canoeing also has more important aspects. Seeing first-hand the effects of pollution, erosion and industrialisation on rivers sharpens one's understanding of the fragility of the environment. One becomes acutely aware of one's own responsibility towards the environment and the devastating results of ignoring this.

The brown waters of rivers in the summer rainfall region are just one of the indicators of the degenerating condition of our river catchment areas. One only needs to read *Men, Rivers and Canoes* by Ian Player to realise how much rivers have deteriorated in the last 40 years. One was able to drink Duzi water in the early fifties and the river flowed through sparsely populated valleys where game and birdlife abounded. Contemporary descriptions of the route make the modern canoeist extremely envious. Gone are the guineafowl and the veld at Musson's weir, the large crocodile that lived in a pool further downstream, and plentiful duiker in the valley. The following description by Mr Wood, an "old timer" in the fifties, illustrates the extent of change and degeneration:

> The river beyond Bishopstowe is still as wild and isolated as I knew it first forty-five years ago. It is a very snaky place, but so long as you don't interfere with the snakes, they won't interfere with you. There is so much advice that one could hand out (to canoeists of the 1950s) that it would take pages. The young men of today, however, don't think much of an old stager's advice and it is a waste of breath to hand it out.

While the environment undergoes a revolution, it seems young men don't change that much!

The Umkomaas is another river that has not escaped the ravages of time. A Zulu *"kehle"* (old man) described the valley to Ian Player.

> He said that wild animals had ceased to be of any significance many years before. In his youth he and his father had hunted leopard that lived in the krantz overlooking the river. When he was an umfaan he remembered white men coming from Richmond and Ixopo to shoot

the crocodile that once inhabited the pool where he had been fishing the night before.

Baboons had plagued the valley dwellers by swooping on the ripening crops and destroying many weeks of toil in a few hours. The baboons seemed to know the women were powerless to act, and only when the men came storming home from a beer drink would they beat a hasty retreat. The tribesmen persuaded a group of white farmers to help, and within a year the baboons had been reduced to one troop. Late one afternoon this troop was surrounded and wiped out with rifle fire...

He (the old man) smiled wistfully and said, "We were sorely troubled by the wild animals, but they gave us much sport and kept us fit when we hunted them. Now there is nothing left to hunt and we all grow fat and lazy sitting in the shade of our huts while the women till the fields."

Nowadays more subtle dangers lurk in the muddy waters of industrial rivers. Now, more than ever, unseen poisons and chemicals find their way into the waters, a problem which is compounded by the use of soaps, detergents, shampoos and other impurities in the river.

Projections on industrial growth rates and future water needs have serious implications. South Africa is a dry country and the storage of water in catchment dams is one way of meeting the demand for water. As demand grows, more dams are built, flooding hectares of useful and beautiful countryside for the sake of increasing industrialisation in a wasteful, power-guzzling society. Conservational living is the best way of coping with limited resources.

Canoeists themselves have a responsibility to the environment. Don't exacerbate the pollution problem. Dropping plastic packets, leaving tin cans behind, littering the river with polystyrene and beach balls and using soap, shampoo and detergents in the river are all part of the pollution process.

As a canoeist one tends to think one can do so much and no more, but we need to go beyond picking up our litter on a canoeing outing. We can add our voices to public outcry at despoiling practices and use our influence in the workplace to enforce environmental controls on activities that damage the environment. Remember that rubbish travels down the arteries of the country on its way to the sea. It is on these arteries that we encounter it, swim in it and drink it. Are you prepared to canoe in the nation's rubbish? We cannot, like the tired canoeist, sit back out of breath and let the current drag us over the falls.

Social responsibility

In addition to a responsibility towards the environment, canoeists have a social responsibility. Leaving gates open, blocking access roads and trespassing onto private land to get to the river alienates canoeists from landowners and makes access to rivers that much more difficult. Canoeists often need help from locals and this will not be forthcoming if you have just flattened a fence, left litter at your picnic site and tramped through a mealie field.

Many of our country's rivers run through black reserves where people own very little and are wholly dependent upon their small patches of maize and other crops to stave off malnutrition. Political feeling is running high in the 1990s and each one of us has a responsibility to defuse the volatile and tense atmosphere. Wandering through kraals and fields does not help. Nor does swearing at the young boys who ask for your hat.

To people who have nothing, the average canoeing party must appear rich with their motor cars, canoes, picnic hampers and multiple changes of clothes. With no access to these luxuries, pilfering becomes a great temptation and is considered part of the redistribution process. Watch your things and never leave your car unattended. Being robbed is a nasty experience, but swearing at every person you see after that will not return your goods to you.

Many of us know the feeling of being a target to stone throwers and our natural reaction is to explode with righteous indignation as a 2 kg killer whistles into the water inches from our heads. It takes humbling self-discipline to turn and wave "Good morning" to your would-be assassin, but it saves you and others from further rocks.

A sign of the times as a paddler skirts an unnatural obstacle in the Umgeni river. (Val Adamson)

A friend of mine once found himself the target of an angry youngster with a rock poised in readiness to throw. With lightning thinking he yelled "Good morning" and the missile was dropped as the youth beamed a toothy smile in reply.

Canoeing action

A sensation unique to canoeists is the desperation of being capsized and trying to right oneself with a roll. Within the canoeist's psyche develops a rare intellectual sensation: the realisation that one is mortal and that there is a fraction of a difference between being a hero and a corpse.

Jerome Truran, one of the best rough water paddlers this country has ever seen, captures the feeling exactly in this description of the first descent of rapids minus 1 and minus 2 on the Zambezi. In the mists of Victoria Falls, it is not only the size of the rapids that frightens one but the eerie sense of timelessness of the falls. The river gods seem ever so near, ready to transport you into the next world. Here where Livingstone explored, we have the cheek to play. Surely the river gods will punish us.

Upside down just after the hole in minus 2, the familiar pressure shock waves coming up at me were the kind that only reflect off a shallow river bed. The horn of rock two seconds after the hole must be close now. I hope I'm not on line.

Roll up — I can't ... the pressure. I can't get my paddle into position. I'm being pushed too far back. It's too strong. Wait until it's past, then roll. Protect your face with your forearms.

I wanted to clear those rocks, I wanted fresh air, I wanted light, I wanted to see the cliffs again, I wanted to be up and out. To grace the fluffy water on the side of the big hole at minus 1 with my shoulder.

I wanted to mock the turbulence and wave at the crowd; to emerge from this helter-skelter. The quiet green pool above the boiling pot needed a hero.

Tearing at my life-jacket the horn penetrated my rib cage and gently committed my heart to the Zambezi. The water turned red and the crocodiles stirred ...

I smiled and knew the quest of a thousand trips had been won. We had found "The Jagged Rocks".

Then of course there is the humour and cameraderie that abounds in canoeing. How can anyone who is not competitive enjoy a long hard flat water race like the Vaal marathon! The answer lies in a sense of humour.

In the large groups that form, break up and reform, wit and insults flow freely. Master canoeist Hugh Raw describes the mood in this experience on the Vaal:

So then we found another group to paddle with and it formed and reformed, some dropping out, new crews joining up. Although nobody talks much, there is an amazing bond that develops in such a group. It is, I suppose, a sense of sharing the load. You have lots of time to study the crew next to you and speculate about them because there is nothing else to occupy your thoughts, Imagine my pleasure when a mixed double joined our group. This girl sat in front and was definitely in control. She had straight golden hair, a lovely tan and the most graceful style I have ever seen. Man, I tell you it was poetry in motion. Paul fell under the spell too because we seemed to keep seeing the lass many times that day, and he kept beautiful formation with her. So under the circumstances we made good time.

The lure of canoeing

To those who know the sport, the lure of canoeing is irresistible. As the rays of the sun flash on the paddle and water droplets tingle on sun-warmed skin, one is overcome with a sense of pleasure. At this late stage in the twentieth century, there is still so much primeval adventure to be experienced and so much to conquer.

The lure of canoeing is nowhere more evident than in Graeme Pope-Ellis's continued participation, at the highest level, in the Duzi marathon. I asked Graeme why, after 15 wins, he still does the Duzi. Surely the pleasure of winning must dim with time? And surely pressures of competition, of always being the favourite that everyone wants to dethrone, must get to him? Yes, they do, he says, but there is more to racing the Duzi than that.

Firstly there is his love for the valley. With its hills and thorn bushes, heat and dust, and the mud shacks which shelter from the heat in the shade of the hills, it has a uniquely African atmosphere. Racing the Duzi has become a way of life; he has to think back to his childhood to remember a time when he was not involved in the race. It has a living atmosphere, as much of a social event as it is a canoe race. If you can play a central part in such an event, why sit on the sidelines? For Pope-Ellis to stop doing the Duzi would be more difficult than to keep on racing it.

In dominating the race for two decades, Pope-Ellis appears to have found the key to eternal youth. This illusory quest, he admits, plays a part in his continued participation. Each win proves to him that he still has what it takes to win, which is immensely satisfying for an athlete in his mid-forties.

But when Pope-Ellis won his first Duzi with Eric Clarke back in 1972, he certainly did not think he would still be winning the race two decades later. "I hoped for three wins." he says. "Each win after that was a complete bonus."

Of these, his first win undoubtedly meant the most to him. "That was in the days when the race was small and uncommercial, but then a win meant everything. It was a hard race and although I have had hard and satisfying wins since, the 1981 race is the only one that has given me a comparable amount of satisfaction."

The joy of white water; Mark Perrow at play in a stopper. (Val Adamson)

The 1981 Duzi was a battle of the giants. Comrades gold medallist Danny Biggs was putting his running to good effect in the low rivers of the early eighties. Much of the Duzi was a running race then, and Biggs proved himself to be the fastest man in the country when it came to running with a boat on his shoulder.

During the race the lead changed hands continuously and for the first time in 10 years predicting the winner was not a foregone conclusion. Spectator interest increased dramatically during the race and a massive crowd gathered to see the finish in Durban. The two only parted company on the flats into Durban when Pope-Ellis pulled away.

Duzi fever

Of all the canoe races in South Africa, the Duzi attracts by far the most publicity. It is the race that all the paddlers want to win and yet it is the race that many of the paddlers deride and curse. Some say it is not really a canoe race at all and refer to it as "a Mickey Mouse event". The running rules out most good canoeists and the canoeing rules out many good runners. The Berg, Vaal, Fish and Breede are more worthy of the good canoeist's attention, and sprinting, white water and slalom are all purer forms of canoeing. The latter two enjoy international competition in these times of sporting isolation, and yet no other event can gain the following or publicity of the Duzi. Its detractors can do no more than accept this, for the Duzi, like the Comrades in road running, is an unorthodox but newsworthy event. This Mickey Mouse is built like Arnold Schwartzenegger.

Big sponsorships, TV and press coverage, commercial involvement and public interest all help to boost the Duzi to a superstatus which no other canoe race equals.

Other forms of canoeing are best enjoyed when not compared with the Duzi. What they lack in sponsorship and publicity is more than made up for in tranquility, intimacy and superior water conditions.

The future

In the 1990s, a new generation of superstars is emerging in canoeing. They might yet get a chance to compete legitimately at international level abroad, and although we have perhaps dropped behind the rest of the world in certain spheres such as sprinting, it will not take us long to catch up with overseas countries.

The international isolation from competition suffered by South Africans in the last decade has hindered the development of canoe racing here. Yet despite this, South African paddlers have still been able to compete abroad, albeit surreptitiously. Gone are the days when a

Springbok team could compete officially in Europe, and this has had an inevitable effect on the racing standard.

It has meant that for the South African paddler there is little point in specialising in any aspect of the sport. It has, ironically, given local paddlers the chance to diversify and enjoy river canoeing instead of spending every moment in a canoe training.

The sport is no longer a small, unpublicised Cinderella affair. Thousands of canoeists now take to the water. It has moved beyond the developmental stage although many changes are still occurring. The advent of plastic canoes and new challenges such as waterfall running have opened up a new dimension to canoeing. It is in this area — where paddlers are attempting the previously impossible — that the greatest changes to canoeing are likely to come in the future. The plastic boat has also been responsible for the growth of canoeing as a leisure sport. At last the recreational side of the sport is becoming as popular as the competitive aspects.

Canoeing, with its diversity and complexities, its problems and pleasures, euphoria and disappointments, is a sport as colourful as life itself. When the rain beats down on my roof and the rivers roar in the valleys, I check my canoeing gear, pack the car and head for a river. Perhaps I shall meet you there.

GLOSSARY

Aerobic exercise – Muscular activity which uses oxygen.
Anaerobic exercise – Intense activity where muscles use fuel faster than it can be produced by oxygen.
Brace – A stabilising stroke where the paddler leans his weight on the back of the blade which skims on the surface of the water.
Break in – Entering the current from a still eddy.
Break out – Pulling the canoe* out of the current into an eddy.
Buoyancy – The flotation fitted or added to canoes to keep them afloat in the event of a capsize.
Bus – A large group of canoes riding in a group.
Canoe – A boat propelled by a single-bladed paddle. The term is commonly used in South African English when discussing kayaks, and is consequently used throughout this book when discussing kayaks.
Diamond – A point at the back of a group where a good wave-riding opportunity exists.
Dumb-bell – A short, single-handed weight used in gym training.
Eddy – An area of still water to the side of the main current.
Ender/"endo" – A rough water acrobatic manoeuvre where the canoe stands on its end.
Eskimo roll – A paddle stroke used to right a capsized canoe.
Feathered paddle – The blades of a paddle set at right angles to one another.
Ferry glide – Using the current to cross the river without getting washed downstream.
Fibreglass canoe – Canoes made from glass-reinforced plastic.
Harness – A carrying device used for portaging in the Duzi marathon.
High brace – A stabilising paddle stroke.
Hip flick – Rotation of the hips in order to bring the canoe upright when rolling or bracing.
Hole – The hollow that exists behind a rock in rough water.
Interval training – A system of training where paddlers alternate between going hard and slowly.
Kayak – A small boat propelled with a twin-bladed paddle. Correctly speaking, all boats used in South Africa in competition, rough water tripping and sea "canoeing" are kayaks. (*also see* Canoe)
K1 – A single-seater kayak.
K2 – A two-seater kayak.
K4 – A four-seater kayak.
L.D. or l.d. – Abbreviated term for long distance.
Loop – Like the ender, but the boat continues beyond the vertical to do a somersault.

* See explanation under "Canoe".

Neoprene	– Waterproof rubber sheeting used to make wetsuits and spray covers.
Pedals	– The rudder control mechanism used in racing kayaks.
Plunge pool	– The deep pool found at the bottom of a waterfall or high drop; usually very deep.
Polyethylene canoe	– Often termed plastic canoe; also called tupperware. Durable rough water boats.
Portage	– Carrying a canoe overland.
Pull-back	– Water on the surface flows upstream, stopping the canoe and pulling it back upstream.
Pulling	– The boat in front providing the initial wave upon which the others ride in l.d.-type canoeing.
Rocker	– The curve along the keel line of the canoe. Rocker can be either curved or flat and affects the turning of the canoe.
Roll	– Reference to the eskimo roll; the method of righting a capsized canoe.
Rough water	– see White water.
Seal launch	– Getting into the canoe on the bank and sliding into the water. This can be done over cliffs or off low banks.
Spray cover	– The plastic material or neoprene "skirt" worn around the paddler's waist and attached to the cockpit of the canoe in order to keep out water.
Splash deck	– see Spray cover.
Spray deck	– see Spray cover.
Stopper	– A wave where water flows upstream on the surface.
T-bar	– A rudder control mechanism where the boat is turned by a bar between the feet.
Telemark (high and low)	Special turning strokes used in rough water canoeing.
Tongue	– A stream of fast water down a rapid.
Turkey	– A derogatory term used in the USA to describe paddlers with little ability who try to do more than they are capable of.
Water bottle	– A bottle or bag containing drinking fluid worn by canoeists.
Wave riding	– Also referred to as "riding slip". A flat water racing technique where a paddler surfs on the bow wave of the boat alongside.
Weir	– An artificially built wall across a river, usually for measuring flow.
White water	– Turbulent-flowing water. The term is interchangeable with wild water and rough water.
Wild water	– see White water.
Wings	– Paddles designed to minimise drag on the back of the blade and increase paddling efficiency.

INDEX

aerobic exercise 55
anaerobic exercise 55—6

Berg River marathon 78—80, 114—6
bilharzia 168
bow rudder 30, 37
brace 33, 34
breaking in 39
breaking out 40
Breede River marathon 117
bridges 158—9
buoyancy 163
Bushman's River marathon 98, 129

canoe polo 123
clothing 15, 163
congestion 159—60
cramps 170
Crocodile River, Highveld 119, 133—4
Crocodile River, Lowveld 120
current 31, 39—41

dehydration 167
diarrhoea 169
draw stroke 34, 35, 36, 37
drinking bottles 103, 105
Duzi River marathon 72—5, 100, 102—7, 126, 177

ender ("endo") 42, 43
Eskimo roll 44—8

ferry glide 40—1
fibreglass 16, 17
Fish River marathon 117—8

grading 143—9
gym training *see* weight training

harness 105
health 167—70
helmets 13—15, 157
hypoglycaemia 167—8

injuries 165-6, 168
interval training 53—5

K1 4—5, 102, 103
K2 5—6, 29—30, 102, 103
K4 7

long distance (L.D.) 30, 78—80, 99—121

Molenaars River 137
Mooi River 128

Natal 125—33

Orange River 138—9

pacing 87
paddles 8, 23, 103
Palmiet River 137
patching 16—17
plastic canoes 1—2
pollution 172
polyethylene *see* plastic canoes
pools 122—4
pumps 10—11
pyramids 53—4

rapids 31, 143—4
repairs 16—17, 19
roll *see* Eskimo roll

safety 157—66
sea canoeing 153—5
slalom 91—7
slalom kayaks 2
slap support 26
slip riding *see* wave riding
spray cover 11, 12, 103
sprint 75—8, 81—4
stability 26
stoppers 161
style 25—6, 48—9, 83—4
sun protection 169

surfing 153—4
swimming 164—5

technique 23—49
telemark turn 32—3
training 50—80, 94—7, 105—6, 152

Transkei 139
Transvaal 119—20, 133—6
trees 160—1
triathlons 150—2
Tugela River 132—3
turning 26—7, 29, 30

Umgeni River 125, 126, 127, 128—9, 131—2
Umkomaas River 108—13, 127, 129, 132

Umzimkulu River 126—7, 128, 130—1, 132

Vaal River 119, 135—6

warming up 84, 87, 89
water bottles *see* drinking bottles
waterfalls 143
wave riding 27—8
weight training 55—6, 64—5, 78, 95—6
weirs 118, 158
Western Cape 136—9
white (wild) water 31, 141—9
wild water racing 85—9
wings 9—10
Wit River 138